Soldiers down through the ages have got together and exchanged yarns and tall stories around the camp fire, in a bar, or among friends at home, during and after service. Not all the items here are humourous, but are here to put on record some events and observations from the Australian involvement in South Vietnam. There are no profound deductions nor strategic analyses, just anecdotes, 'funny' things and similar from a personal level.

There is nothing here from the Australian advisory effort 1962-71, and only a little about the RAAF and RAN.

Generally speaking, the Australian sense of humour differs from that of other nationalities, though those societies have many similarities to Australia. Australian military humour is often dry, with no respect for rank or position.

These few examples are included to place on record some incidents from the Vietnam era.

The decision by the Australian government to commit troops to the war in South Vietnam was made despite lack of enthusiasm by the senior ranks in the Defence Force. The Royal Australian Navy was about to accept a new class of US-built destroyers and aircraft; the RAAF was in process of accepting new fighters, bombers and transports. All these items were paid for by the Australian government and budgets were allocated and locked in; there was no extra for warfare.

The Army was in process of expanding to train and employ the young men soon to be conscripted for two years of national service in the Army, because of fears of military aggression by Indonesia. President Sukarno of Indonesia cultivated the communist bloc and his regime seemed to be heavily influenced by them and the national Communist Party, the PKI, was the second or third largest in the world.

Australia had been in a dangerous situation in World War 2, when in 1942 Britain could not send any land, air or sea forces to the region to take part in operations against the Japanese until 1945. Every available Australian battle-ready unit, fighter or bomber or naval ship in December 1941 was deployed in support of Britain in Europe or North Africa. When the British did announce a return to the Pacific area it was with the assumption that a Briton would be in command of the Commonwealth forces, but this was strongly refuted by the Australians, who had long experience actually fighting the Japanese.

In the early 1960s Britain obviously was soon to depart South East Asia. If Indonesia became communist, the perils of 1942 would be small in comparison.

So it did not take much deep thought to deduce that the wartime US-Australian alliance should be re-created, and assistance to the US effort in South Vietnam would be an insurance payment against the possible need to ask for help against a communist Indonesia.

To provide trained soldiers in case of Indonesian aggression, a two year term of National Service was introduced in 1965. Selection was by a type of lottery, in which some birthday dates were drawn and the 19-year olds born on that date were required to present themselves for military service. This selection method was not popular with anyone.

In early 1965 it was almost a daily news item that reported yet another defeat of the South Vietnamese government forces by the Vietcong. It seemed that soon the South would fall to the communists and the strategic disaster of 1942 would be in place again. So the political decision was made to commit combat units to South Vietnam.

The decision to commit Australian forces was an important step for the government and the nation. In every other war in which Australia had been involved, it was as part of a British Empire or Commonwealth force. This was the first time Australia had 'gone it alone', though there were earlier similar steps.

The Australians had long been aware of their position as a small population, 99.9% of which was Anglo-Saxon-Celtic- Nordic stock, in a big continent on the edge of the teeming millions of Asia. Japanese military expansion had long been a cause for concern. After the Russo-Japanese War of 1905, the chiefs of the newly created Australian federal defence force asked their counterparts in London for detailed reports. The brusque reply was that Australia would be told what it needed to know when it needed to know it, when London decided anything was necessary.

The result was creation of the Australian Intelligence Corps in 1907, the first such in the British Empire. Previously, as need arose, a small Intelligence component would be formed for use in a British campaign, usually after one or more of the military disasters that so crowd British military history. To counter later Aussie claims to have created the first professional national military Intelligence organisation in the Empire, the British came up with Walsingham, who formed a similar organisation to support Queen Elizabeth 1 against plotters and the Spanish. Australian response to this was usually a laugh.

In 1941, when it became clear that Australia was low on the priority list of British concerns, the newly established Labor government of John Curtin made independent approaches to the USA on military and diplomatic matters. This did not go down well in London, but was necessary, as events proved.

But for Australia to independently commit to a war was a big step. The Royal Australian Navy had always been considered a part of the Royal Navy's Pacific force, and recommendations for medals were compiled and sent to London, where it was decided what action would be taken – if any award was to be made and what it would be. RAN ships flew the RN ensign – but after 1965, flew the Australian version.

On the domestic side, the 1966 federal election was fought on the main point of involvement in South Vietnam, and resulted in the biggest defeat to that time for Australian Labor, who lost ten federal seats. Later, as the war dragged on without signs of progress as in the World Wars, public support slackened. Meanwhile, the members of the Army, Navy and Air Force served as required on operations.

So here are some yarns and memories from those days. There are many more with other veterans.

70 Days later

When the 1963 year-long courses at the School of Languages ended, there was no relevant employment for some of the graduates and three Vietnamese linguists requested a posting to a new infantry battalion formed near Adelaide, South Australia; they had never been to that part of Australia. On arrival, they found that this battalion had been formed for the purpose of assisting British and Malaysian forces against the aggression of Indonesian military in the '*confrontasi*' campaign; President Sukarno did not agree with the creation of Malaysia.

The battalion commander would have preferred Indonesian linguists, but was happy to have three men who were graduates of the language school. One was injured in a car accident, another was discharged for political activity, and the third stayed, happy to prepare for war service against the Indonesians, as there seemed no prospect of any such in Vietnam.

On one training exercise, in March 1965, the linguist and the battalion commander were waiting for a helicopter. The daily news was of disasters inflicted on the Army of the Republic of Vietnam (ARVN). The battalion commander made frequent visits to headquarters in Canberra and was well-informed of the situation. The linguist asked if Australia was going to be involved in South Vietnam and the lieutenant colonel assured him that it was not, as

'It is a losing war there.'

Seventy days later the linguist was standing in a big grassy expanse at Bien Hoa, now in the First Battalion, The Royal Australian Regiment (1RAR), looking at tropical rainstorms, wondering how to erect his hutchi with no trees around, and if the Vietcong were planning anything.

Speak more slowly,
please

When the Australian involvement in South Vietnam increased from 100 advisors to deployment of a combat formation, the rifle companies of 1RAR were delivered by overnight flights of chartered Qantas Boeing 707s. On the first flight were two linguists, one of them the man mentioned above, graduates of the School of Languages. Both were keen to speak to Vietnamese other than their tutors.

The 707 landed at Tansonnhut at dawn, and the troops waited while the cargo was unloaded. Standing nearby was a local in white overalls, obviously a supervisor of some sort. The linguists approached him, greeted him in Vietnamese and asked how he was today. The man looked at them without sign he understood. They tried again, speaking slowly and carefully; no reply.

One linguist said in English to the other, 'He can't understand a word we say.'

The supervisor smiled and said in English, 'Are you speaking Vietnamese? I am Manuel. I am with Philippine Airlines.'

Devious government and military planners?

The prejudice-holders and conspiracy theorists of the Left live in the strong belief that Right-wing governments and military hierarchies are always planning for involvement in a war somewhere.

The Australian involvement in South Vietnam was not the result of such machinations, as shown by the hasty deployment of the 1RAR Group, and by the basic fact that no one knew how long this tour of overseas duty in a war zone would be.

So from the start there was uncertainty at personal level, especially for arranging family matters. All this led to an unhealthy climate of rumours, fed partly by those who enjoy starting a rumour and waiting to see how long it takes to get back to them, and in what form. Also, friends and wives back in Australia sent snippets of information acquired in Canberra, none of which was helpful.

When an official statement of the length of duty in South Vietnam was announced as 'one year' the rumour mill continued. Nothing the battalion command did put an end to this nonsense.

Clean living troops

1RAR was surprised to find on arrival that the commander of the US 173rd Airborne Brigade (Separate), to which they were attached, had decreed that no alcohol was to be consumed within his brigade. This has to be among the most fatuous orders from the Vietnam War, and came from an officer who was a veteran of WW2 and Korea.

Alcohol was easily available in the clubs on the adjoining Bien Hoa air base, in Bien Hoa city, and in Saigon, not to forget villages in the area. There was no way that a brigade of US paratroopers, with Australian infantry and New Zealand artillery attached, was going to conform meekly to this order.

One notable event was when a 1RAR platoon commander was at the air base officers' club, had consumed enough drink to make him feel invulnerable, and decided to take some beer back to his troops. He bought a case of beer, took it outside, put it down in the middle of the street, sat on it, and awaited the next vehicle. A US Army jeep arrived and the officer in it asked if he could help, to be told to drive to 1RAR, which was done.

Unfortunately, the US officer was the brigade commander himself. The platoon did not get the beer but the young officer was night duty officer for a month.

Eventually, the order was rescinded, on the convenient excuse that as the Aussies had 'Royal' in their unit title, and it was the custom to drink a toast to the health of Her Majesty Queen Elizabeth II on the occasion of the battalion birthday, an issue of beer would be permitted. This was followed by official permission to have alcohol in the brigade.

However, the happy event was spoiled for many of the Aussies when the beer supplied was Hamm's, from San Francisco, that had nothing like the taste of beer enjoyed by Aussies, and even some hardened drinkers could not finish a can. Later more acceptable brands arrived and were enjoyed.

First impressions
When the first rifle company of 1RAR arrived at Bien Hoa, to a large area cleared of rubber trees, the stumps had not been removed. For months Aussies could be seen limping after bruising a shin on a stump in the darkness.

Behind them was the busy airfield; to the front, some bush and long grass; to one side, a forest.

Reacting as trained, the Aussies established a company position and started to dig fighting pits. On the extreme left of the position, under a sapling, sat a US paratrooper, looking out at the grassy expanse. Two Aussies assumed he was on the right of an adjoining US unit and walked over to ask about fields of fire.

Disillusionment set in when the paratrooper knew nothing about arcs of fire or anything else about the position, and could only say, without interest, 'Better ask the sergeant over there.'

When darkness came, the Aussies put on their webbing, got into the pits and went into the evening 'stand to' procedures in the operational area. Nearby Americans called to ask what was going on, and when told it was 'stand to', nodded, said, 'OK' and continued with their activities.

The Aussies were surprised to see the neighbouring US cavalry unit, resident for a few weeks, did nothing to indicate it was in a war zone. Lights shone everywhere; vehicles went to and fro, headlights bright; truck doors slammed; radios blared music; people shouted. Paratroopers, cigarettes lit, casually walked across the Aussie front, heading for the bright lights of Bien Hoa.

Later there was a shot from the US position. It was reported that a sergeant and a trooper had an argument and the sergeant settled it by shooting the trooper.

When 1RAR battalion headquarters arrived, the first command post was in a tent with pallets for a floor. Artillery support was from the US artillery in the brigade, and two officers arrived with their maps and talc overlays to liaise with the 1RAR commanding officer and senior staff. As the US officers left, one was heard to say to the other,

'Isn't it great to talk to people who understand artillery?'

A couple of the Aussies who overheard this immediately wondered if such a comment was a reflection on the ability of US units in the brigade.

An immediate impression concerned the great differences in personal appearance. The US troops all wore the same pattern uniform designed for the tropics, with big pockets on the trouser legs and a neat long shirt worn outside the trousers with useful-sized pockets, as well as a good tropical boot with canvas sides and eyelets to allow water to be squeezed out after immersion. It also had a flexible steel plate in the sole to protect against the legendary sharpened poisoned stakes allegedly placed everywhere by the devious guerrillas. All this was the envy of the Aussie soldiers.

A US unit on parade in field uniform looked like a professional military outfit, all with the same appearance.

Officer Commanding
D Company 1RAR,
Second-in-Command,
two platoon commanders
(1RAR)

1RAR wore standard Australian issue, which was a motley of designs for shirt and trousers dating from World War 2, with a variety of shades of green that depended on the age of the shirt or trousers and if they were originally khaki for desert use dyed green in separate batches. The trouser leg thigh pockets were too small to be useful for anything except a folded map or note-book.

There was some anticipation in 1RAR when an issue of gear for tropical war service was announced. It was assumed that somewhere there was a warehouse full of good stuff. Disillusionment set in when each man was issued with puttees and a dilly bag, a small drawstring cloth bag for carrying toilet gear on a voyage. That was it, the extent of military holdings for deployment.

The Australian ankle boots on issue sometimes were of a reddish leather, the standard Army boot until 1949, and a constant joke was that sometimes the boots were older than the young soldier who received them. The red boots had to be painted black with leather dye and have black boot polish applied.

Similarly, the Australian bush hat – 'giggle hat' – came in a variety of designs and shades of green.

An Australian unit of the time on parade in field uniform looked like a group of men dressed by a philanthropic charity organisation after a flood or fire – different shades of green, different designs and no two bush hats the same in appearance.

The 1RAR commander achieved a small measure of fame when he effortlessly tore a shirt in half in the presence of the visiting Minister for the Army, himself a Korea veteran, to demonstrate the poor quality of government issue available. The bureaucrats, of course, replied to this by alleging that the soldiers took with them to Vietnam only old clothes and kept the good ones for 'best' use.

Since 1945, the Australian government had been able to avoid all the expense of providing modern field uniforms by having the units deployed to Korea or Malaya clothed for winter or the tropics by the parent force there, the USA or Britain.

Soon the 1RAR soldiers were wearing a mixture of US and Australian uniform, particularly the US boots. A useful trading item was the Aussie slouch hat, and another was the bush hat, as the US Army did not have this on issue.

There was only one other item the Americans wanted from the Aussies – the canvas shower bucket. This handy item allowed anyone to have a shower if there was a convenient tree or something from which to suspend the bucket. There was nothing like it in the US inventory.

US military showers

After some days in the grassy expanse at Bien Hoa, 1RAR was told showers would be available. Carrying personal weapon, towel and soap, the Diggers climbed aboard US trucks and set off down the dusty road to shower. There was a degree of culture shock. Rather than an arrangement of pallets for flooring and shower buckets available, with water heated in tubs or a 'donkey' that released the equivalent hot water when a bucket of cold was poured in, the Aussies came to a large canvas screened area, divided into two large sections.

In the first, clothes were removed and placed on benches, with weapons. Then a whole batch of men walked into the next area, where shower nozzles were arranged at intervals around the perimeter; no taps or personal water controls.

At one end a US soldier controlled the water flow, and he announced that water would be on for 30 seconds, off for a minute, on for another thirty, off and everyone would leave, dry off, dress and depart, soapy or clean; no lingering.

The Aussies accepted this quietly but there was a sort of stunned silence, that a man could not even enjoy a shower, but was processed as a small item in a big machine. This was military administration in the big league.

The media

TV and journalism crews from Australia, the USA and other parts of the Free World were looking for stories continually, and over time the attitude of many of them alienated the Aussie soldiers, while their superior attitude and the spurious assertion 'the public has a right to know' alienated many of the commanders.

1RAR had experiences with the media early in the tour that made the Diggers reluctant to speak to them. Sometimes it was only by the place names in the news item that the soldiers recognised the operation as described by the journalists. US soldiers were far more relaxed with journalists, and some became exasperated with the Aussies, so one complained that after several days with the Australians in the field, the only personal remark heard was from the sergeant-major, who said he must be getting old as he stood and stretched.

At the completion of the first operation by 1RAR there was an unfortunate fatal accident with a hand grenade on the harness worn by a soldier, when the pin caught on a section of truck body, was pulled as he dismounted, and the grenade detonated, killing the US truck driver and three Aussies, with others wounded. A photographer arrived and was carefully taking photos of the dead and wounded until the battalion adjutant noticed and smacked the camera out of the man's hands, with a warning to stop, and to think of the families of the casualties.

A well-known Australian journalist was banned from the battalion, to his fury, for publishing details of a forthcoming operation despite an undertaking to with-hold such detail until the operation began.

Ba's Cantina
At Bien Hoa 1RAR was given a Tactical Area of Operational Responsibility (TAOR, spoken as 'tay-or') extending north from the battalion position to the southern bank of the Dong Nai River. On the left of this was the Cong Thanh District capital of Tan Phu and on the right the TAOR of one of the US battalions.

Once Australian patrolling and ambushing quickly imposed control over the TAOR life in Tan Phu became much more relaxed. Before the rival of the 173rd Airborne Brigade, the area had been dominated by the Vietcong, and the US advisors in Tan Phu had watched, from their compound, the local Army of the Republic of Vietnam (ARVN) company trounced by an enemy squad within 1,000 metres of Tan Phu. The advisors did not dare go on foot more than 500 metres east of the town. But this soon changed with the arrival of the US and Australian units.

In Tan Phu the local restaurant and bar became known as the 'cantina', from US Western movies, as it was on the edge of 'Indian Territory' and almost everyone carried guns into the bar. The Vietnamese for a mature or married woman is '*ba*', so the place became 'Ba's Cantina'.

The Australians had many reasons to visit Tan Phu, to liaise with the Vietnamese authorities and the US advisors or to play volley-ball. Unfortunately, all the advisory team except the officer in command in 1965 were killed on later tours of duty in Vietnam.

What is this for?
The variety of weapons carried by everyone in the area was a matter of soldierly interest. One day in the Cantina a young, respected, Australian platoon commander became interested in a version of the US M3 .45-calibre 'grease gun' carried by one of the local troops, and asked to look at it.

This was the version without a cocking handle, but only a hole or recess in the bolt into which a finger was placed and the bolt pulled to the rear before firing.

The young officer pointed the barrel upwards, opened the feed plate cover, saw the finger-hole, asked, 'What is this for?', was told and pulled the bolt back, then released it to a chorus of 'No! No!' as the bolt went forward, picked up a .45 round, took it into the breech and fired.

Silence; the sound of falling pieces of the photo of the deceased husband of the bar owner, from its place of honour above; the sound of fast footsteps as all the Vietnamese soldiers found something to do elsewhere; then an Australian voice, 'Four beers, please.'

Take as much as you like,

but eat all you take

Until the 1RAR rear echelon arrived on the aircraft carrier HMAS '*Sydney*', the Aussies ate at kitchens operated by the 173rd Airborne Brigade. This was a pleasant surprise. The Australian Army ration scale was tightly controlled and administered by Australian Army Catering Corps (AACC) NCOs and officers, traditionally called 'bait-layers' after the bushmen who laid poison baits for wild dogs.

There also was the saying, 'Who called the cook a bastard? Who called the bastard a cook?'

But, in an Army supply system with its roots in the frightful conditions of the trench warfare in 1915-18, North Africa 1941-42, the South West Pacific in WW2, and Korea, with the problems in just getting food and ammunition forward, strict attention to volume was necessary. So the Australian ration scale was for one egg a day, a small but adequate piece of meat, vegetables, bread, condiments, and similar.

The Aussies at Bien Hoa in the early days were astounded to find the US cooks placed food on a man's plate as long as he paused in front of them, rather than in the Aussie system where one piece of whatever it was in the tray was carefully lifted out and placed in the dixie or on the plate.

The Aussies were very pleased to be told,
'Take as much as you like, but eat all you take.'

Then the Aussie cooks arrived and it was back to the old system.

Why not give them a whole egg?

In 1RAR the caterer was a Warrant Officer Class 1, product of long term service in peace-time, promoted beyond his level of competence, comfortable obeying the rules in Australia, set in his ways, and incapable of adapting to the wide range of foods available for the asking at Bien Hoa.

On one of the early daily visits to the food supply location, one of the US troops queried the small number of eggs requested, and was amazed when told the ration was one-third of an egg per man per meal, and asked,
'Why don't you give them a whole egg?'

We don't eat that stuff

The 1RAR soldier was impressed with the rich variety of food available from the US system, especially the small cans of fruit juice, flavoured milk, and all the meats, salad makings and vegetables. The US soldier then queried the lack of these items, and was told by the WO1 that,
'We don't eat that stuff.'

A 1RAR soldier present piped up with, 'Yes we do!' and was told to 'Shut up. I'm the Warrant Officer Caterer here!'

However, the situation was soon resolved by the battalion commander having a brief talk with the WO1 and the food presented in the 1RAR Messes improved considerably.

We have to eat this?

Until the Australian supply system caught up with the situation of having to support a battalion-plus force in South Vietnam, US C-Rations were provided. The size and bulk of a US ration for one meal was a surprise to the Aussies, as an Australian 24-hour pack was the same size.

The inclusion of a tin with a small bread roll, and others with pound cake and pecan nut cake was of interest, but some of the other contents soon had the Aussies in agreement with their US allies. Ham and lima beans, chicken and noodles and others were not popular but eaten. Cigarettes in ration packs was not something the Australian government would provide.

Before every operation, outside the 1RAR tents a pile of unwanted rations would accumulate – tins with a bread roll, pound cake and the rest. Disposal of these was a problem, as it was not policy to give tinned food away to civilians, as the enemy would confiscate it.

They are out there, look at the lights

1RAR had sentries on the machine gun positions on its forward perimeter. One night a section commander was called by his soldiers – there were small flickering lights moving through the trees out in front. The corporal looked, and, sure enough, tiny lights were there. It was obvious the people carrying them did not want to be seen and moved carefully through the bush in the dark; something was being planned.

It was decided to call down some artillery on the location; the lights went out. Later they were seen again; more artillery. This time it was decided that the battalion would stand-to, much to the displeasure of those watching the outdoor movie.

More artillery was called in but the enemy seemed to be determined to carry out whatever their task was, as after each short bombardment there would be a pause, darkness, and the lights would re-appear.

Finally a patrol went out to see who was there and if any bodies or equipment could be found. There were no bodies or equipment, but soon the fireflies lit up again and began flying around.

Body count
The 'body count' of enemy dead after an action was devised in the early 1960s by the US Military assistance staff as a way to determine the effectiveness of the South Vietnamese armed forces in action. The enemy made great efforts to remove all the dead, wounded and items of equipment after an action, partly to demoralise their opponents, who would be left with no or very little sign a battle had been fought.

High enemy body counts in revolutionary warfare are a sign that many people are joining the anti-government organisation; low body counts indicate the opposite.

Body count became a major reporting procedure to indicate success, and, human nature being what it is, figures often were increased at command levels to improve the 'appearance' of a formation.

It soon became obvious that the figures often were inflated, and this, with other revelations, led to lack of trust in the US command, especially at briefings for the media. The hapless briefing officer could only relate what was presented to him, but often enterprising journalists had been at the battle site then travelled to Saigon to the briefing – and refuted the official version.

Within the US-Free World military, body count remained a major sign of success though it was recognised as faulty.

1RAR noticed soon that while it might be in the same operational location as the two US battalions, sometimes finding little sign of enemy or having little contact, the other battalions were reporting substantial body counts.

On one operation, 1RAR was sweeping an area on the south bank of the Dong Nai River, and the US units were on the north bank. While crossing an expanse of grass and small shrubs, D/1RAR came under fire from a recoilless rifle on the far river bank, and high explosive rounds began to explode around them. The pace was quickened to reach a forested area, no one was harmed at all, the fire stopped, and normal staff work at brigade showed that D/1RAR at location 'x' was at the same location fired on by the US cavalry unit of the brigade – who opened fire on an area where friendlies were – and who claimed 20 enemy killed in action, from a firing position on the far side of a wide river. This was a complete fabrication.

We have fire power
– use it!

The commander of the US 173rd Airborne Brigade began to realise the nature of early operations – fleeting contact in most cases, with little to show for it. But his tactical solution to lack of positive results was not practical.

He proposed that every man in the leading platoon fire 100 rounds in the direction of the contact.

It was quickly pointed out that this was extremely dangerous to the men up front if all that ammunition came from those in the rear. The tactical solution was not adopted.

Time is not to be
wasted on the landing
zone

1RAR soon found the US Army helicopter units had a far more professional attitude to operations in a war zone than the RAAF in peacetime Australia. The RAAF procedures evolved from the parsimonious RAF policies in Malaya, where the enemy did not interfere with airlift matters. In South Vietnam the Vietcong took active steps to counter heli-borne operations and often shot down helicopters on or close to landing zones.

The lengthy RAAF procedures involved the helicopter landing firmly, but no infantry moved to it until the pilot was satisfied and gave a thumbs up, returned by the senior soldier waiting, the doors were opened, the pilot and soldier confirmed the sortie destination, the soldiers boarded, carrying their packs and webbing gear, fastened their seat belts, checked by the senior soldier, the doors were closed, more thumbs up all around, and flying commenced.

The US Army procedure was for the helicopter loads – 'sticks' – to wait along the landing zone at the correct distance, the Hueys arrived with doors slid back or removed, touched down, the first two soldiers ran around the nose and boarded from the distant side while the others climbed in, no-one fussed with seat belts and some sat on the floor, after seven seconds pitch was pulled and flight began. On arrival the helicopter settled for about five seconds, troops jumped out, and lift-off began, depending on the leader.

There was no doubt about the professionalism of US Army helicopter units in a war zone.

Why don't they say that?

There were marked differences in some word usages. On an early operation with night helicopter activity the aviators were confused by Australian references to use of torches to guide the helicopter to the correct spot. The Americans understood 'torch' to be a burning piece of wood or tightly bound sticks, and wondered why these were used. The Australians used 'torch' to refer to a battery-powered hand-held electric light; an American 'flashlight'.

The US issue torch was a superior item, with a useful clip to attach it to military gear, and a supply of coloured lenses, powered by dry batteries. The Australian issue of the time was the equivalent of an old-fashioned light that clipped onto a bicycle, used an inferior cardboard-covered battery that was vulnerable to moisture, and had no coloured lenses, but did have a movable shade to limit the amount of light projected.

It's on the tube

1RAR received some US weaponry and delighted in most of it, though the AR15/M16 was not popular with everyone because of jamming, separated cases and split stocks. The M79 was popular from the start.

The cartons of M66 rocket were delivered, unloaded, and the US sergeant prepared to climb back into his jeep. One Aussie platoon commander asked, 'Aren't you going to show us how to use them?'

The reply became famous: 'It's written on the tube, man.'

And so it was – complete instructions for use; a situation unheard of in the Australian Army.

Take a message
to brigade

Early in the 1RAR tour of duty with the US 173rd Airborne Brigade, the air base was warned of a possible enemy attack at night, and a state of alert was declared. All brigade units were in darkness; it was raining heavily; in the distance some sort of battle was going on and the noise of explosions could be heard.

A corporal in 1RAR was called to the command post and told to take a message to brigade. The corporal realised at once that this was potentially dangerous – travel through a blacked-out brigade spread over a wide area, driving along roads guarded by trigger-happy US troops and South Vietnamese of unknown ability, when enemy were expected, in heavy rain.

He told the driver to go slowly and be prepared to leap out at any moment in case some frightened Yank or Viet opened fire.

So they set off, creeping along with only parking lights on, the corporal calling out *'Uc Dai Loi'* (Australian) and 'Australians', past silent tents and buildings, constantly hearing the sound of weapons being cocked, and the mind-focusing heavy clank of a .50-calibre Browning heavy machine gun readied for action; got lost; drove around in the dark and rain, and found brigade headquarters and the command post.

The corporal was relieved to be there, but knew the equally dangerous return trip had to be made.

The US officer on duty looked surprised to see an Australian corporal appear with a small brown official envelope for him. The officer opened it, read the message, and asked the corporal if he knew what it said. The corporal said he did not know; he was the messenger. The officer showed him: 'From: 1RAR. Nothing to report.'

Yes, they are our
allies, but...

The commander of the 173rd was surprised to see that 1RAR submitted requests for far more barbed wire and steel pickets than the other two battalions, and, aware that the Aussies did not seem particularly worried about the Vietcong, questioned the extra defence stores.

He was told that these were for use between 1RAR and the New Zealand artillery battery to prevent New Zealand theft of Australian equipment.

Oh, ours is painted
green
The New Zealand artillery battery had asked for a fork-lift to carry 105mm ammunition from the delivery area to the guns, but the parsimonious New Zealand government refused.

Acting on the principle that 'God helps those who help themselves', and being on the perimeter of a modern US air base, some of the Kiwis took one of their trucks to the air base, drove around, saw an unattended fork-lift, drove it onto the truck and sped off to the gun position. Like much of the ground equipment on an air base, the fork-lift was bright yellow.

The US Air Force did notice the loss of a fork-lift, and investigation soon showed that it had last been seen on a non-US type of truck heading to the 173rd Airborne Brigade area. USAF military police went to the area and asked at all the units.

The NZ artillery commander did not know of the theft, and when the USAF MPs were taken to his tent, he could say honestly that he knew nothing about a stolen fork-lift, then noticed his sergeant major, standing behind the MPs, frowning and staring fixedly at him, with small sideways nods, then past the tent came a fork-lift, gleaming in a new coat of green paint. He quickly recovered to assure the investigators that his unit had one such machine, but it was green, like all army equipment. The USAF men accepted the word of a New Zealand commander, saluted and left.

The NZ officer exhaled and said to the sergeant major, 'Never do that to me again!'

Now do you
believe us?

The 1st Battalion, 503rd Parachute Regiment, had a heavy contact in November 1965, the first such experienced by the 173rd Airborne Brigade. The battalion was caught in low ground by outnumbering Main Force enemy, but fought its way to high ground, consolidated as best it was able, and held off enemy assaults.

Forty-nine troopers were killed and many other wounded. Enemy dead counted were about 400, and later captured documents indicated losses were around 700. This sort of body count had not been reported before the battle, and there was some lack of belief at higher headquarters.

To prove the point, a cargo net was brought in, spread on a convenient piece of ground and enemy dead were piled on it. A helicopter picked up the gruesome thing and lowered it onto the grassy patch at brigade headquarters.

Uh-oh. I have to eat some of this
The job of processing the dead troopers of 1/503rd devolved onto D/1RAR, and the bodies were flown to their landing zone in the condition they were picked up on the battlefield.

D/1RAR's task was to remove all military issue items, including ammunition and rations, but to leave personal items in the uniform pockets. This was a grisly task, but had to be done. A taxi-rank of Hueys formed and as six bodies were ready in body bags, the lead Huey came forward, collected its cargo and left for Saigon.

The day was hot and humid, but by the time it was over it was lunch time. A platoon commander and a corporal were walking away when they passed a pile of C Rations. The second lieutenant said that it was lunch time, and stooped, picked up a ration tin and walked on. Not to be outdone, so did the corporal. The lieutenant opened his tin, which contained sweet biscuits and popped one into his mouth with a big grin, looking at the NCO.

The corporal had not read the label on his tin, opened it and was confronted by a sight that he did not want: chicken and noodles. Some of the dead paratroopers already had displayed the results of death in the tropics and had been fly-blown....

The corporal knew he had to eat some of the ration tin or never hear the end of it, so manfully took out his spoon and chewed on the unappetising mess.

I saw it myself,
lieutenant! They
use rain water!

Early in 1RAR's deployment, a Land-Rover with passengers went to Saigon and overstayed their visit, so it was too late to return to Bien Hoa that evening. They had checked in with the headquarters in Saigon, but needed a story to account for their late return.

The driver had it all figured out. During the afternoon wet season downpour, somehow rain water must have entered the fuel tank, so making the problem.

After arriving back at the Bien Hoa airbase, the base perimeter road had to be followed to reach the 173rd Airborne Brigade position, and then on to 1RAR.

At one of the small airfield defence posts manned by South Vietnamese, in a Beau Geste Foreign Legion-style fort built in the French days, there was a big roadside puddle, where the Land-Rover halted. The driver opened a petrol tank filler cap and scooped up a canteen cup of water, then poured it in. One of the passengers noticed the interested post defenders, staring down at this amazing sight – water going into a foreigner's vehicle! He mentioned this to the driver, and suggested a powerful take-off.

This was done, red dirt sprayed from the tires and the Rover leaped forward. Behind them the entire garrison of the fort ran out to the big rain puddle and tasted the puddle water.

The beer

French cultural advances had not included chilled beer, despite several attempts by her German neighbours to bring home this lesson. The two local brands of beer in South Vietnam were drunk when nothing else was available.

The best-known was '33' – *ba-muoi-ba* in Vietnamese, shortened to 'barmeba' by the foreigners. Embroidered '33' patches designed like the official logo were on sale and decorated bush hats, jackets and vests.

The other was *'Bier La Rue'*, with the logo of a panther's head, and so became known at once as 'panther's piss'.

With their usual concern about health and hygiene and avoidance of disease, the US authorities tested the beers and found them to be unfit for human consumption, with '33' including a large amount of formaldehyde. This did not concern the young drinkers from overseas, who were at the age of considering themselves as immune to harm.

When the desire for cold beer was understood by the locals, they took a pragmatic solution to the problem: put ice in the beer. This was not to the liking of the customers, but tolerated. A common sight was a large glass of beer with ice chunks floating in it.

What the drinkers often did not see was the delivery of ice to the bars. The large blocks of ice arrived in the back of a 'Lambro' – small commercial vehicle based on the Lambretta – or a small truck, and slid along the floor of the bar. It was broken into big chunks and placed in containers for later use. Sometimes in the ice would be various pieces of debris, such as bottle tops, grass or straw, pebbles and so on, all indicative of the health and hygiene practiced at the ice-works.

Finding this stuff in one's drink was accepted as part of the adventure of serving in South-East Asia.

Vung Tau Bars and hotels – 1970

Vung Tau was only one city in South Vietnam with a strong military presence, both US-Free World and government.

In 1970 the official list of hotels, bars, restaurants and massage parlours in the city environs was 165. Of these, 37 were listed as 'Out of Bounds' to US-Free world military personnel.

Why is that officer wearing a beard?

When the Australian commitment to South Vietnam was a small number of advisors, travel to and from was via Singapore and Malaysia, with use of military facilities there.

One officer, a graduate from the Vietnamese faculty at School of Languages, was posted to the advisory team, and arrived in Singapore with a beard. Nothing was said at first, as there was an assumption that he might be going to some special operations role in Vietnam. But a senior officer noticed and asked why the beard, to be told the officer was growing it as a protest because he did not agree with Australian involvement in the war. His onward travel ended on the spot and he was returned to Australia.

Working for the US Imperialist aggressors?

It was decided to put an air base at Tuy Hoa, with the expected benefits to the local farmers of a ready and constant market for their fruit, vegetables and salad components, so creating a steady source of income, increased prosperity and generation of a pleasing glow of affluence derived from personal effort – the basic concept of US democracy.

The brutal reality was that the farmers and families flocked to the air base, to work for assured wages, meals, protective clothing for some tasks, and the possibility that a daughter might marry a rich US serviceman. Very few farmers owned the land they worked, but were tenants of absentee landlords. Work at the airbase meant an end to that relationship, to debts, the vagaries of weather, hard physical work in the fields, among pests and critters, at the mercy of the land-lord's agents, government officials, Vietcong officials, subject to terror, forced labour for the Vietcong, and the possibility of becoming collateral damage during an operation by or against the Vietcong.

One of the great enduring promises of the communists was that the farmers would own the land they worked and the workers the factories. The attempt to expand the revolution into Thailand failed because Thai farmers owned their land and every citizen had the right to a personal audience with the King to present perceived wrongs.

The opportunity to leave a landlord-tenant relationship was too good to ignore.

Cultural differences

The Aussies and Kiwis of the time used the word 'boy' as a greeting and in normal conversation. It was very soon found that 'boy' was regarded by the Negros ('African American' had not been invented) as an insult, with connotations back to the days of slavery in the South, when a black male of any age was called 'boy'.

With the usual US intolerance of other cultures, there was a complete refusal by the Negros to accept that another society in everyday conversation might use a word they disliked, and reacted angrily.

The Aussies also soon learned of the poor standard of education provided most of the Americans. They knew a lot about their home State, some more about the USA and almost nothing about the wider world. The general attitude was that the USA was the most powerful nation in the world, the US dollar the most powerful currency, everyone wanted to move to the USA to enjoy its benefits and politicians from anywhere else went to Washington DC to beg.

The Aussies took quiet enjoyment from the number of Americans who said they already had been to Australia, enjoyed the ski-ing, the beer, Vienna and had cruised the Danube. They also commented on the style of English 1RAR used, in that none of them seemed to have a Germanic accent.

A US citizen who later lived in both countries said that the USA was inwards-looking and Australia was outwards-looking. This would apply to other powerful societies over the ages – Greeks, Romans, British and French – and smaller nations.

Another assumption was that any item of US equipment in use by another defence force had been given it at the expense of the US tax-payer, and there was some polite disbelief that Australia and New Zealand paid the USA for every item in use.

As an aside to this, when the RAAF team to accept the first Lockheed C-130 'Hercules' transports arrived at Lockheed, they were puzzled by the casual reception and basic accommodation provided. In conversation with one of the office staff, one RAAF sergeant asked what was the significance of the coloured tabs on the file covers of the Australian order for C-130s, seen on the desk. The Lockheed office worker explained that the colours were a designation of the type of purchase, and that this set of colours meant the aircraft were to be provided under an aid agreement at the expense of the USA. The Aussie quickly said this was wrong, Australia was a cash customer. A check proved this to be so and the whole attitude of Lockheed changed – much better accommodation, a very friendly attitude from all Lockheed staff, cars and transport for recreation provided.

One aspect of the Australian military that the US officers envied was the batman, in that each Australian officer had a soldier assigned to take care of his daily 'domestic' requirements, such as supply of clean clothes, digging a fighting pit, preparation of a tent in the field, and passing on to the troops some orders. The batman was a volunteer, and a source of 'inside information'. He took his turn on the radio, and had a full day, either in base camp or in the field. His activity allowed the officer to devote all his time to military matters. The US military did not have this system.

The Aussies soon came to the conclusion that there were several different 'types' of US servicemen. There were very professional officers and senior NCOs, with a wide range of experience; capable men who were masters of their chosen profession.

Many others, regardless of rank, seemed to be acting in the role of what they thought was required of a US paratrooper, a US paratrooper sergeant, or a US paratrooper officer. Mandatory items were a cigar and a declared love for bourbon.

Bravery was commonplace, but the desire to bring the Vietcong to battle and then use firepower and bravery to achieve complete victory resulted in many casualties. One company in a US battalion in the 173rd Airborne Brigade had a complete turnover of personnel in six months to January 1966.

Legs and airborne

The US paratroopers in the 173rd Airborne Brigade had the usual disdain for those not qualified as parachutists, called by them 'legs'. The brigade had a number of non-parachute small units attached and it was proposed to have a parachute course to qualify those who wished to do so. As a matter of administration, 1RAR was notified, and battalion headquarters was swamped with lists of names. There were so many Aussies wanting to be paratroops that they could not be accommodated and the idea was dropped.

The Americans were stunned to learn that Australia had a very small airborne component, with no Regular airborne unit on the battle order, and that parachuting was permitted only to keep a cadre available.

World War 2 and post-1945 experience showed that injuries suffered in parachute operations were about the same for hurriedly trained units as for long-time airborne units, and the Australian government quickly seized on the point that this showed there was no real need to provide the expensive aircraft, parachutes, facilities, training and maintenance of skills for parachute units, let alone the extra pay for airborne personnel. If a parachute operation was planned, experience 1941-45 showed all that could be gathered in time of need and units selected for the brief training time necessary.

Cleanliness is next to Godliness - 1

The change from peacetime attitudes to what was normal in a war zone sometimes meant painful adjustment for some with the mind-set,
'If it moves salute it; if it doesn't, paint it white.'

The Australian M113s of Prince of Wales's Light Horse (PWLH) – a title that delighted the US allies at Bien Hoa – arrived in South Vietnam from the comfortable barracks with all the attention to cleanliness in Australia, and found mud, dirt and dust were normal. Some PWLH crew commanders became upset at the dirt tracked into the nice clean vehicles by the uncaring infantry, who actually stood on the nice clean seats to see better out of the top hatch.

It was a common sight in the early days to see a broom, brushes and a dust pan in the M113, and a busy crew member sweeping. This did not last long and common sense triumphed.

Cleanliness is next to Godliness - 2

The peacetime emphasis on cleanliness affected the RAAF. On a training exercise in Victoria, a RAAF Huey helicopter crew actually had a boot scraper at the helicopter and insisted the infantry make an effort to remove dirt from their boots before boarding the nice clean flying machine. Also all packs and personal equipment had to be removed and carried in the hands, to avoid dirt marking the nice clean webbing of the seating in the Huey.

Darwin Awards – 1965

The annual Darwin Awards was not around in 1965, but some events certainly qualified for inclusion. A 1RAR soldier sent out as sentry on an early operation presumably had drunk from the 'Darwin Awards waters' because he decided there was no one around and thought he would pass the time reading. A cautious Vietcong moving towards the position of the Imperialist aggressors could not believe his good fortune: a foreign soldier engrossed in a book. He checked his safety catch and took careful aim.... The Aussie died of wounds.

Be careful what
you wish for

Outside the main gate to the Bien Hoa air base were various stalls selling cigarettes, fruit and drinks. One cigarette seller was a boy, whose real job was to record the vehicle unit identifications and identification numbers and time of travel, to allow the Vietcong to compile all this to try to determine habits and itineraries.

The boy's father had been killed in the war against the French and the family continued against the Saigon government and now against the Americans. The ideal was to remove oppression and establish a free society.

The young fellow grew up and later was a combat soldier in the Phu Loi Battalion, survived the war, and joined the police. But he realised that, as at other times in Vietnamese history, in 1975 the Northerners had not arrived to unify Vietnam but to impose an occupation, and Southerners were to be kept in their place. When his attitude drew attention, he knew he had to leave. The alternative was arrest and disappearance to a jungle camp.

He fled Vietnam as a boat person, and after time in a camp in Malaysia, eventually arrived in Australia as a refugee, to start a new life. In letters home, he was full of praise for his new country, and described the freedoms and opportunities available, all the things for which he and his father had fought, but which were denied after victory. He had to stop writing home when his mother advised him to do so, as the security police had read all his letters before delivery, and had visited her.

War Service

The realities of war service showed that some people were not capable of adjusting and there were a few failures. Some of these people were sent back to Australia, but when the battalion returned in June 1966 and gathered for a march through the streets of Sydney, it was found that, as the Army was expanding to cope with the influx of National Servicemen, most of those sent home had received several promotions and now outranked those who had remained in South Vietnam.

One second lieutenant who remained with 1RAR for the full tour had a less than good tour of duty. On the first operation into War Zone D he managed to shoot himself accidentally in the foot, and was even included in the commemorative book produced by the 173rd Airborne Brigade for all who were there, photographed limping to a casualty evacuation point.

His immaturity resulted in infuriating his platoon sergeant, who lost his temper and punched the young officer in front of the platoon, which resulted in a court-martial and punishment.

The young officer was moved to a number of positions within the battalion but failed at each one, and eventually was seen around the battalion shirtless, in shorts and boots, with a wheel barrow, planting banana trees, while soldiers returning from operations, laden with pack and weapons, walked past to their tents. It remained a mystery to some why he was not returned to Australia and requested to resign.

One rifle company commander was determined that his company would protect him from the enemy, and when assigned an area to search on the sweeps into an area where little was known of the enemy, he retained two platoons with his headquarters while one did the searching, and at the first sign of enemy would halt, and form a company defensive position while the lone platoon coped. He once sent one of the Australian linguists 800 yards (metres) alone through the bush from the headquarters to the platoon to deal with any language aspects. He was shuffled out of that position to the staff and company command devolved to the far superior second-in-command, who was in his third war and had been promoted from the ranks.

Another officer, who considered himself the social superior of all those junior to him found very oppressive the lack of privacy at the original all ranks 1RAR latrine at Bien Hoa, and would use a vehicle of his sub-unit to go to brigade where separate facilities existed for officers, senior NCOs and soldiers.

Saigon – you can
see it for miles

None of the South Vietnamese cities had been designed to cope with the increases in population, nor the arrival of large numbers of foreign service personnel and the numerous units. Saigon had been described as a beautiful colonial city, and it had been so.

But from the beginning of the US build-up more people, buildings, vehicles of all kinds and refugees had crowded in and the tree-lined streets were clogged with traffic.

Travellers approaching first noticed a milk-chocolate coloured cloud on the horizon, and realised that under it was the city, and they would soon be breathing that mixture of fumes from diesel and petrol, wood fires, charcoal and kerosene cookers.

Later the trees were removed from the streets to allow for the increased traffic. One more sign of the pleasant colonial tropical city was gone.

Expensive? Yes, but
what the hell, it's war!
The first operation by 1RAR was a simple shake-down overnight sweep through an area south of Bien Hoa to both allow the battalion to practice air mobility and to see what was there.

A four-man team from the US radio research unit (RRU) with radios arrived to accompany 1RAR, to listen to Vietcong radio traffic. There was no secret about this and what they were to do was known to all who saw them among the Aussies.

During the operation they picked up radio transmissions from a Vietcong who was watching some Aussies, and from his remarks it was possible to deduce his location. It was decided to fire artillery on his position.

Sure enough, he reported that artillery was falling close to him and that he would have to move. He did, but again his remarks allowed his location to be deduced and again he had to flee to avoid artillery. This happened all afternoon, and his increasingly desperate comments provided amusement for the Aussie and Yanks at 1RAR headquarters.

The RRU team that usually deployed with 1RAR became good friends, to the extent that a common greeting between RRU and the Australian linguists

was,

'I'd rather have a sister in a whorehouse than a brother in (1RAR/RRU).'

The watchers

It became a common thing for the RRU operators to report that someone in Bien Hoa city was watching everything that happened in the 173rd Airborne Brigade area, and at the helicopter landing zone. When battalions were being lifted out, the observer would   notify his listeners 'that x-number of helicopters were flying west' or that 'x-number of big trucks with soldiers have arrived at the helicopter area'.

The 173rd Airborne Brigade never did find out if the observer was found.

I don't like going
there after dark

Unlike the US battalions, at Bien Hoa 1RAR settled into a dispersed position, on the reverse slope of the ridge that went down to the Dong Nai River. This kept exact locations out of view of observers on the far side.

From the air, the US units were laid out neatly in a nice military style. The tents in 1RAR seemed to be scattered haphazardly, but in reality were situated as part of a plan that had the defences able to fire across the front of neighbouring companies in case of attack. The only 'military' style of layout was at the battalion headquarters area, where a small parade ground was cleared and tents and marquees arranged around it, with a vehicle park next to it.

No Vietnamese were allowed into the battalion area without escort.

At night the battalion was in darkness, though all around were fully lighted US and South Vietnamese units, an airbase, and a city. US and South Vietnamese did not like this arrangement, nor the idea of infantry waiting in the darkness for someone to stumble on them, with dire results.

There were several mortar attacks on the air base – the really valuable target – but there were none on 1RAR. Though an alert would sound, many in the battalion did not bother to get out of bed and watched the flashes of explosions at the base. Next day there would be no sign of much damage, as the huge USAF machine kept right on operating. The loss of a couple of aircraft meant nothing.

Which Army are you?
On the successful operation in January 1966, when 1RAR captured the Vietcong headquarters for the Saigon region, General Westmoreland came to visit. The usual order to tidy the area went out, but Westy's helicopter descended low over part of the 1RAR location, and the down draught disturbed everything movable.

Westy walked along the path from the landing zone to 1RAR HQ and came upon the RRU site, where there was some disarray, a jeep with US markings, some soldiers wearing US uniform, some wearing Australian, and some wearing items of both.

He stopped, looked around, and asked one of the RRU soldiers, 'Which Army are you?'
'US Army, sir!'

Westy looked around again and shook his head.

He then turned to one of the Australians, who had a sweat rag around his neck, pointed to it, and asked what it was, then, when told it was 'a sweat rag, sir', nodded and said,
'Uh-huh, keeps you warm at night, huh?' The Aussie shook his head.

The media
After 1RAR had been some time in-country, among the media visitors was a middle-aged female from a well-known women's magazine, eager to report on how the bronzed Aussies were coping. It was decided to show her the benefits of civic action projects rather than military operations, so after admiring the flower beds around one tent, she was taken to the nearby village of Ong Huong.

The various projects were shown and the happy smiling faces of the locals were what the woman had come to see. She noticed a little boy with a mug that came clipped to the bottom of the army canteen, and that there was something written on the mug.

In a sweet voice suitable for speaking to young children, the woman leaned over, and took the mug from the boy, with,

'What have you got written there, little boy?'

Unfortunately the little boy had learned English from soldiers, and reacted instantly with,

'Get yer c---t-scratchers off me f-----g mug!'

'Ohh, little boy!'

No discussion

The intense aerial activity around the Bien Hoa air base was always of interest to the Aussies of 1RAR. F-100s took off trailing flame from their afterburners and the very air shook; transports of all types circled in and out; flights of 50 or more Hueys, with armed gunship escorts flew in and out; US Navy and USMC fighters sometimes arrived and departed.

The aircraft that generated much interest were the black U2 reconnaissance planes that silently appeared, sped down the runway and climbed steeply away, to some unknown location, and as quietly returned and were towed into a hanger to which visitors were turned away.

The very presence of the U2 was secret, but it could be seen by everyone in the area.

Some Aussies had a quick introduction to the serious nature of the restrictions placed on reporting anything about the U2. Happening to be on the air base perimeter road when a U2 appeared, the opportunity to take photos was seized, but any quiet satisfaction did not last long. Whoever reported the photography was never known, but suddenly big blue USAF vehicles would appear, loaded with Air Police, who did not enter into conversation but stopped the Aussie Land-rover, searched for the camera at gunpoint, took it and smashed it, then drove away.

I've had enough

1RAR normally stood-to at dusk, in case the devious enemy managed to gather an assault force and try to break in at the start of night. One evening, two corporals in the Intelligence Section could see a figure approaching from D Company, and it looked like a man with all his military equipment. As the shape neared they recognised a well-known soldier, a proud Englishman (see below) who was good when in the field but had a low boredom threshold in base camp and had acquired a reputation for finding alcohol anywhere.

Sure enough, he was drunk. He had come to the Section to get a map and compass and intended walking to Phnom Penh, to the British Embassy there, to request a return to England, as he was fed up with the Australian Army.

The corporals pointed out that it was nearly night, he had to somehow cross the Dong Nai River to even start towards Cambodia, and it would be best to wait until morning. This was agreed; he went to sleep and when he woke walked back to D Company.

This man's army career was given a positive aspect when a couple of the warrant officers discussed him, as it was intended to not renew his engagement at the end of the current term – he was a disciplinary problem. It was decided to see how he reacted when given some responsibility, with one stripe and the rank of lance-corporal. This worked wonderfully, and by 1968 he was a good sergeant, and later a warrant officer. He still liked beer.

The pineapple seller
On the first operation into the Ben Cat area, the ground forces halted in the town to allow B-52 strikes to hit ahead of them. The local merchants soon realised there were commercial opportunities here and began selling fruit and cold drinks.

When the B-52s had gone the advance continued out of town and into the bush and rubber plantations to the west. 1RAR settled into a position in the rubber trees; night came.

It was bright moonlight, but under the rubber trees all was dark. The Australian policy of no lights, noise or movement at night was in force; all was quiet.

A group of three Vietcong arrived and casually walked towards the darkness – their previous experience had been against government forces and so far this night there had been nothing to show that they needed to do anything different.

There was one short burst of machine gun fire and all three were hit. One took some time to die, calling for his mother. When dawn came, there was one of the smiling pineapple sellers from the day before among the dead.

You want what returned?

In all previous wars, Australian fatalities were buried overseas, in well-maintained cemeteries set aside for the purpose. In South Vietnam, no such arrangements had been made, and the first Aussies killed were flown to Malaysia for interment at WW2 war graves locations. The government of the day adopted a bureaucratic response to requests from families for the remains to be brought back to Australia for burial by friends and family, and announced that the expense of such would be borne by the family. This was despite the fact that RAAF C-130s made regular flights to and from South Vietnam.

Eventually, after fellow soldiers and private citizens raised the money for some such returns of remains, the Treasury was forced to meet the costs. In 2015 negotiations began to return to Australia the remains of those buried in Malaya.

Darwin Awards
– 1965 – 2

Despite the action in which the pineapple seller was killed, and that on previous operations, there must have been some element of Darwin Awards in the air. Next morning two soldiers from the company position where the three enemy were killed were sent out as sentries.

Of course, the actions by people who qualify for a Darwin Award cannot be understood. This pair decided to have a little picnic. Not only did they get out their Hexamine heat tablet stove and all the coffee powder, pound cake and the rest, but did so in a cleared piece of ground outside the bush that should have concealed them. One fool actually was sitting with his back to a tree, facing away from the enemy, back towards the company position.

Again, a cautious Vietcong approaching the rubber plantation could not believe his good fortune. He aimed, fired and fled.

The fellow sitting with his back to the enemy was hit in the buttocks, managed to get back to the company position and collapsed. A patrol that swept out to the scene came upon the evidence: Hexamine cooker, coffee, sugar, cake, and the bloodstain against the base of the tree. In certain other armies there would have been severe punishment imposed. How the fool explained being wounded in the buttocks when on sentry was not known.

That will not work here

A source of irritation for the US officers and soldiers, from the arrival of 1RAR at Bien Hoa, was the constant pointing out by Aussie soldiers of the lack of US expertise in patrolling and ambushing. Since 1942 the Australians had concentrated on mastery of jungle warfare, small unit operations in difficult terrain. This had been boosted by recent successful experience against communist terrorists in Malaya.

The US Army had a global reach and was a massive enterprise, with some base camps that held more units than the entire Australian Army, and was organised and trained to fight huge operations against large enemy forces in Europe, or, perhaps, Asia. Here was this tiny Allied force that could not even provide each man with identical uniforms with the effrontery to criticise.

Frequent orders from 1RAR headquarters for the troops to cease being critical of and uncomplimentary to the US Army and 173rd Airborne Brigade went unheeded.

The 1RAR Intelligence people worked closely with the US RRU linguists. During one conversation about counter-revolutionary warfare, one of the RRU guys came up with what he thought would be the argument to shut up the Aussies: that the US Army did know how to fight guerrilla warfare campaigns, because it had defeated the Indians (now Native Americans).

This had the opposite effect – a laugh and the point that the Indians had been defeated in winter campaigns, caught on the prairies or hills, in the snow, when their camps had been raided, tepees and contents burned, horse herds shot and buffalo wiped out to deprive them of food and hides. There would not be snow in Vietnam, the Vietcong did not rely on horses or buffalo and did not live in tepees.

It's a living

The insatiable demand of Intelligence for information provided a living for many South Vietnamese. Payment for agents was provided freely, was nontaxed by the local government, and, due to turn-over in US Intelligence staffs, there was little analysis of the value of information provided. The astute South Vietnamese learned what the Americans wanted to know about, so set off into the outside world and returned with the needed detail.

In at least one base, Long Binh, an Intelligence/S2 'shop' was in plain view of the ARVN living quarters across the road, yet 'agents' openly arrived and departed, on their motorbikes, carrying away bags of good things from the PX.

At the First Australian Task Force (1ATF) field base at Nui Dat, in Phuoc Tuy Province, one Australian Intelligence Officer was less than trusting of the value of agent reports and completed an analysis of the content of a large number of Intelligence reports received from higher headquarters. The basic facts revealed that most of the information from 'agents' was from the same couple of industrious fellows who rode around the circuit of S2 offices with the product of their imagination and sold it to each office in turn, so that along the line a report was received from several places, so tending to 'confirm' the content.

One ludicrous result was the report of a Vietcong Atomic Division outside Saigon.

On another occasion, the 1ATF Intelligence Officer presented the commander with bad news – the Aussies were surrounded by huge forces of enemy; annihilation was nigh. To the commander's question of what should be done, the reply was to do nothing as none of it was true.

Fun at the beach
The beach at the seaside of the city of Vung Tau was 'reserved' for the local people, but the distant 'Back Beach' on the ocean side of the isthmus was for the foreigners, who were more accustomed to the surf and conditions. This was where the Australian logistics base was established and where troops came to relax for a few days away from the Nui Dat base and operations.

An Aussie warrant officer on his second tour of duty was at the beach, with many others enjoying things there, and noticed a small group of Aussies, trotting along in double file, under control of a corporal. They halted not far away and began to do organised exercises, and then to play beach volley ball, with the corporal supervising.

The warrant officer recognised one of them as a fellow member of the battalion on its first tour of duty. This fellow recognised him too, and left the group to say hello. The corporal noticed this but did nothing.

The warrant officer asked what unit his old friend was in and was informed it was the same one. The next question was whether this was a platoon on rest, and the answer was a surprise: they were all prisoners at the military police jail, down at the beach itself for some healthy exercise.

When asked what he had done to be in jail, the reply was that on return to Nui Dat from the battles at fire Support Base 'Coral', instead of a rest, the battalion was set to work cleaning and tidying before a visit by the Prime Minister, John Gorton.

With the well-known aptitude for individual thinking by the Aussie Digger, some had decided there were enough people around to do the necessary cleaning-up, packed small bags and walked to the heli-pad, where helicopters flew in and out frequently. There they simply asked for a lift to Vung Tau. When their money ran out, they reported to the logistics base, took their punishment – back at Vung Tau! – and gave no trouble.

You have three
to six seconds
Many servicemen returned from a day in Bien Hoa or Saigon furious at the loss of an expensive camera or watch. The favourite trick of camera thieves was to snip the slim shoulder strap of the camera, and run. Watches could be taken by grabbing it and twisting hard to snap the slim steel pins in the strap at the shoulder of the watch.

The thief, sometimes a child, would run, often into a bar, toss the item to whoever was behind the bar and keep running out the back entrance, to disappear in the maze of passages.

One of the US advisors at Tan Phu, outside the Bien Hoa airbase, became fed up with the blatant theft of items after his camera was stolen. He bought the case for a camera, then took an M26 grenade, and carefully placed it in the case with the pin out, but the striker lever held by the camera case. He then walked around Saigon playing the tourist, camera carelessly hanging from his

shoulder. Sure enough, he felt the small pressure on the strap, then nothing.
He kept walking and in due course heard the explosion…..

Just relax, just relax
A wounded Aussie had a catheter inserted to allow urine to pass while he was
bed-ridden. When his bladder became painful he complained to the hospital
staff, who said he only had to relax and urine would pass freely. He tried to
relax, nothing happened; pain increased.

After a couple of days, with no urine appearing in the container and the
soldier still complaining, with a visibly expanded bladder, it was decided to
see if there was a fault with the catheter, so it was withdrawn…. And found
to be intact, in that the end had not been clipped off and urine could not
enter. The soldier said that he felt vibration as the volume of urine sped out
of his body.

RPG – what it
really means
It has become usual for 'RPG' to be given as 'rocket propelled grenade', but
this is incorrect, though the letters fit conveniently the description. The
origin is Russian, 'ruchnoi pulemet grenate' - 'squad level grenade
launcher.

There are also the RPK and RPD light machine guns, for the Kalashnikov
and Degtaryev weapons. No one suggests they are 'rocket propelled'.

Cultural differences – 2
The cultural differences were evident in the way in which soldiers off-duty
behaved in the bars and hotels in Bien Hoa, Saigon and Vung Tau. Many of
the Americans seemed to believe that 'being popular with girls' meant
cultivating the approval of the bar girls, who were there simply to extract as
much money as possible from the customers in the shortest possible time.

When the Australians went on leave, they tended to remain in their unit
groups, drank beer, swapped yarns and enjoyed time off with their mates.
The girls were tolerated, used quickly for sex, and mostly ignored – there was
no prospect of a long-term relationship.

The girls and the bar made much profit from the 'Saigon tea' they drank,
allegedly alcoholic, but actually weak tea. When the Aussies were reluctant

to enter into this arrangement, they were unpopular, called 'Cheap Charlie', and 'Ucdailoi cheap Charlie' (*Uc Dai Loi* = Australia).

Someone, probably an Aussie, composed a song to the tune of 'Knick knack, paddy whack, give a dog a bone, this old man is rolling home'. The currency was commonly called the piastre, from the French time, shortened to 'p'.

> *Ucdailoi cheap Charlie*
> *He no buy me Saigon tea*
> *Saigon tea cost many many p*
> *Ucdailoi he cheap Charlie*

55 Days – something
different always

In 55 days on operations in November/December 1965 and January 1966, 1RAR was involved in four separate operations in widely differing locations in South Vietnam involving very different techniques in each. The success of these operations demonstrated the high degree of flexibility it is possible to achieve with well-trained soldiers, experienced NCOs and good commanders.

The first operation required a sudden move by air to a distant rural area, the La Nga valley, in Binh Tuy Province, to secure the rice harvest for the people's own use and not have it taken by the enemy; then a further sudden air movement to a different area to search for enemy combat units. There was a return to base for Christmas, followed by an airlift to another completely different type of terrain, with searches in swamp, rice paddies and canals; then a quick move to another location where the battalion landed under fire, defeated the enemy guard force of several battalions and captured a major headquarters, followed by a week exploiting a captured tunnel system while coping with continuous enemy attempts to penetrate the battalion perimeter.

During those 55 days 1RAR took part in airmobile operations across several different types of terrain, infantry-armoured advances and attacks, and perhaps the most demanding on the individual soldier, tunnel exploration and related activity. The battalion was led by three different Australian officers during this time.

In Binh Tuy, 1RAR moved on foot through the bush south of the enemy-occupied town of Chinh Duc and prepared an early-morning attack from the far side, led by D Company. The platoons surprised the enemy and in a free-flowing series of flanking moves and attacks bounced the Vietcong back; the other rifle companies entered through the initial gap and spread out through the town, forcing the enemy out into the bush. This involved fighting through streets and houses against a defending force on its home ground, with the Aussies all the while moving the population out of their homes and shepherding them to the rear.

No training had been done for this type of operation, but the battalion applied common sense and discretion to the effect that only one civilian was killed and one house destroyed but the Vietcong force was routed. This success generated compliments and visits from various US commanders who admitted that their procedures would have resulted in destruction of the town with air and artillery as soon as resistance was met.

The battalion's next task was an attack on Vo Xu, further along the road into the La Nga valley. The battalion used different tactics, deceived the enemy with feints on the flanks, and C Company, mounted in Australian M113s, sped up the road, through the town gate and into the square; the rifle companies again cleared the streets and homes. The rest of the operation consisted of securing the valley for the harvest, finding enemy supply caches and civic action events.

Strong enemy forces had been reported south of this area; the brigade flew there, and separated into allocated search areas. A heavy contact was experienced by one US battalion but little was found by the Australians. Christmas was spent at Bien Hoa.

On 1 January 1966 the brigade flew to a completely different area - the canals, swamps and rice fields of the Mekong Delta, searching for enemy base areas and armed forces. Here movement and searching techniques across water-logged country required immediate adaptation by all ranks. The third CO arrived in this series of operations.

This operation in the Delta was followed immediately by an airlift to secure an area and capture an enemy headquarters, which was found to be defended by three main force battalions of Vietcong – experienced combatants equivalent of regular troops.

1RAR was under fire as it arrived on the landing zone, and soon all four rifle companies were in action, with events somewhat flavoured by friendly fire from enthusiastic US helicopter gunners flying past and US artillery, who diligently fired twice the serial on their program to prepare the 1RAR landing zone – once before arrival and once after the battalion was on the ground.

Again, the population had to be removed from the battle area while the defending Vietcong units were forced out by section and platoon actions. The extensive tunnel system was found and exploration went on for the next week. The enemy knew the area and the tunnel system, and there were constant small actions as they infiltrated the battalion perimeter, both above and below ground. Rank meant little in the tunnel searches – only slim people could pass along the narrow tunnels and men of larger size simply could not enter them.

This situation certainly had not been covered in training, but the battalion dominated the area and captured large quantities of material, most important of which were the documents from the enemy headquarters for the entire region. 1RAR was resentful that the operation was ended when there were areas yet to be searched and the location of the HQ leaders had just been given by a surrendered Vietcong.

Later, two more big operations without the Australians and 173rd Airborne Brigade were launched into the same area. Neither the Free World Military Assistance Command (MACV) commander, General Westmoreland, nor his chief of Intelligence, General McChristian, mentioned this important 1966victory in their end-of-tour reports.

At no time did the Vietcong, the 'home team' on the home ground, come close to defeating the US 173rd Airborne Brigade (Separate) and 1RAR in any of these operations.

Each of the three commanding officers of 1RAR issued orders for these operations, requiring very different techniques from the soldiers, NCOs and officers and each time results were a success.

Later in the tour 1RAR defended a US engineer unit building a road, during which a Vietcong regimental attack was deduced to be in preparation and was defeated, and also 1RAR successfully defended the large field headquarters of the US 1st Infantry Division using Australian tactics and procedures.

At no other time in Australia's involvement in the Vietnam War did a single battalion with supporting arms cope with so many different requirements in such a short time in successive operations over such a large area with different types of terrain against well-armed enemy on home ground. This is all to the great credit of the Diggers, NCOs and officers of the 1RAR Group and to the reservoir of experience and common sense within the unit.

Bar girls
The girls working in the bars officially were waitresses, and no government official would admit in the slightest that any Vietnamese woman would work as a prostitute, especially for foreigners.

Girls worked in the bars for a variety of reasons – to support their family, to make a living, as a sign of rebellion against officious parents, or to pay off a debt incurred by a parent or grandparent.

There were some sad stories, and many of the girls accepted that it was their fate to be forced to work in that way, but did so with resignation.

The power of the US dollar meant that some girls who did work as a waitress or cashier could be forced to go with an American who desired the girl, had the money to buy her from the bar owner or manager, ignore her pleas, and return her after use, usually much changed, embittered, and a suitable recruit for the Vietcong.

A well-known Vietnamese story was *Kim Van Kieu*, the account of the life of the girl of that name, who suffered great hardships in her life, including time as a courtesan, but who achieved happiness in a traditional 'good news' ending.

Another was a tale of a young Vietnamese girl who fell in love with a young French officer, but who betrayed his defence post in the struggle against the French, in obedience to parental demand – which took precedence over personal desires.

So many of the girls accepted that it was their fate to be working in a bar. Some were thrifty and bought buildings, became business managers of their own fortunes and provided for their parents. Others gambled away everything they earned.

Others again, married with a family, worked in the bars and massage parlours and steam baths in a purely business relationship, with no sexual activity involved.

Here be dragons
The incompetence of the South Vietnamese government and military stemmed from several sources. The French had not created layers of local people to administer the colonies, as did the British in theirs, but used French citizens for almost every job or position, and unless a Vietnamese abandoned his cultural heritage and lived as a Frenchman, with citizenship, he was a member of the faceless majority.

When it became obvious that control had to be handed to Vietnamese, accelerated promotion came for those in the military; sergeants became colonels in a short time, with the equivalent in civilian occupations.

President Ngo Dinh Diem assumed office, and, in a series of hazardous operations smashed the various forces opposing him, and established a court of officers and politicians whose hold on office was decided by him.

With the age-old desire to not report bad news to the head of state, the situation in the countryside was falsified and the increase in support for the Vietcong, with assistance from the North, was disguised. Casualties meant there had been fighting, but when areas had been reported as peaceful, the alternative was to continue to send false reports and do as little as possible.

Consequently, when General Westmoreland had to begin operations to halt the successes of the VC/NVA, he had first to establish a basis of solid information on what was and was not on the ground in the provinces.

The NATO classification of information began at A1, information from a previously reliable source confirmed by others, through to F6, could be true but unconfirmed by any other source. Much of the ARVN information was in the lower grades and frequently F6 – about the level of the medieval map-makers, with 'here be dragons'.

When the US 173rd Airborne Brigade (Separate) went to Binh Tuy Province in November 1965, the local ARVN reported that the La Nga valley was held by the Vietcong, the villages supported them, were defended, and fierce fighting could be expected. The government forces apparently did not know that only seven kilometres away there had been a Buddhist revolt against the Vietcong, that the people in the valley did not support them, and when US-Australian forces arrived enthusiastically gave information on enemy personalities and where food was cached.

The flag pole

The national flags of the USA and South Vietnam flew from flagpoles all around the area and air base at Bien Hoa, as well as in the villages, towns and cities. It was decided that 1RAR would have a tall flag pole, and as the battalion was on a ridge overlooking the air base and city, would be visible from everywhere else in sight.

While the battalion was out on operations the plan was made, the flag pole designed, and construction began. The finished product was laid out on the ground and work began to raise the pole to its full impressive height as the battalion arrived back.

The battalion sergeant major (RSM), a respected soldier who was first in action against the Japanese in July 1942 at Kokoda, had warned that the metal piping of the pole was not strong enough to support its own weight vertically, as it was water pipe and not intended to carry weight.

But he was over-ruled by the officers concerned, who ordered the pole raised.

The ropes tautened and ran through the pulleys, and before the eyes of the returning battalion the flag pole rose to its majestic height, stood a moment, then collapsed into a graceful S-shape.

The officer responsible looked at it for a moment, turned to the RSM and said,
'All right, RSM, get it removed.'

The koala bears

One corps in the Australian Army that benefited from Australia's involvement in the war in Vietnam was armour. The nature of Australian military involvements after 1945 had not included armour or cavalry, and after 20 years had passed the crude infantry referred to armoured people and units as 'koala bears' in that, like the animals, they were not to be exported or shot at.

Armour also was equipped with the 52-ton British Centurion tank, designed to fight the lethal German Panther and Tiger of the Third Reich, and the hordes of Soviet tanks if war came again to Europe.

The Centurion was so big and heavy that it could not be easily moved out of the southern state of Victoria, and there was the sad result of trying to do so by army landing craft that revealed at the moment of truth, at the docks, when it became known that the ship's access door was too narrow for the tank. This was a design fault of an elementary nature that took time to rectify.

But eventually the tanks were brought to South Vietnam and proved a success beyond expectations. Infantry disrespect turned to acceptance and praise.

Where are you from?
Until 1982, British citizens could serve in the Australian Defence Force or public service without the requirement to become Australian. Two such Brits were in 1RAR.

One was a very proud 'Pom', as British migrants were termed by Aussies. In a conversation, the proud Pom stated that he did not believe in changing nationalities, and if a person was born in a country he or she remained of that nationality. The other disagreed and said that he had migrated to Australia, married an Aussie girl, and their children were Aussies, he lived in Australia, paid his taxes there and considered himself an Australian.

'*Never!*' said the first Pom.
'If you are born in England you are English, always and forever! Born in Germany, always a German! Born in France, always a Frenchman!'

'Just as well I wasn't born in a stable,' was the quiet reply.
(Actually said in February 1966, in the field.)

The rice cartoons
that backfired
Early operations in 1965 were forays into the field to establish a base of information on what, if anything, was there. South Vietnamese information

was found to be almost worthless. Food caches were evacuated if possible, for redistribution to the local people, and military trucks brought in for this task.

Some amusement was felt at the disappointment on the faces of the Vietcong who would arrive to check what had happened at their 'secret' sites. This resulted in taunting messages and cartoons being left for them to find, showing grinning South Vietnamese (ARVN) soldiers on top of trucks overloaded with bulging bags of rice and road signs pointing to the nearest town and ARVN military unit. An invitation to a hearty meal with the ARVN was included, much to the merriment of their troops present.

However the Vietcong did not return the humour and after one successful evacuation of a big rice cache, and the usual invitation, to Tan Uyen, the place was subjected to a fierce mortar barrage.

Medication –Aussie style
In 1965-66, Australian battle casualties and those who became ill were treated at US medical facilities. It was noticed by the US medical staff that though the Aussies were dispersed among the wards according to the type of illness or wound, they did not appear to be in the dining areas. Investigation showed that 1RAR at Bien Hoa was sending trays of good old Aussie sandwiches – 'sangers' – each day, and these were much preferred to the US cuisine at the hospital. As the sandwiches were nourishing, this was accepted as a quirky Aussie matter.

However, there was anger from the medical hierarchy when it was discovered that 1RAR also was sending insulated containers with beer and the happy Aussie patients were mixing medication with alcohol.

You'll be going back
on Friday
South Vietnam was divided into four Corps Tactical Zones (CTZ), numbered from the north. The US 173rd Airborne Brigade, at Bien Hoa, was in III CTZ, where that headquarters also was located.

As the US-Free World commitment to South Vietnam was to assist in defence of the Republic of Vietnam (RVN), copies of operation plans had to be provided to local RVN headquarters.

It soon became obvious that the enemy in target areas was informed of operations before the US and Australian troops arrived. The 1RAR linguists found that the Vietcong had gone around and told the local people about the coming operation, and to disobey any orders from the RVN. The linguists were surprised to find that the locals even knew how long the operation would last, and when the foreign soldiers would return to base.

Filthy lucre

South Vietnam was one of the countries whose currency had no value outside its borders. The USSR was another. To work against the acquisition by illegal means of US dollars, the military introduced military payment certificates (MPC) for use in certain countries within the military establishment. Military personnel leaving could change a certain amount, depending on pay for rank, length of time in-country and so on, when departing. MPC was not to be used outside bases, and an official exchange rate was advised. Changing money by individuals at a different rate outside bases was illegal.

Human nature being what it is, there were many locals and foreign soldiers, of many ranks, who changed money illegally. People on the street would accost soldiers with a muttered offer to change MPC; it happened in bars and restaurants, everywhere foreign soldiers were to be seen. With MPC and a friend with access to the US post exchange (PX) system, valuable things could be bought and passed into the civilian economy.

The great danger to those involved in this was when the pattern or design of MPC was changed. This was done with far more attention to secrecy and security than for military operations – well, money was involved!

There were tales of great wailing and even suicides when MPC was changed and some people allegedly were left with hauls of valueless paper that yesterday had the potential to bring in millions in real worth.

Silver wings

In the US airborne community, an operational parachute drop is shown by a star on the parachute badge, and this brings some prestige to the wearer. The 173rd Brigade deployed on operations by helicopter, which was far more flexible than parachutes, but the desire for an operational jump persisted.

The opportunity presented itself in late 1965, for Operation *'New Life'*, into the La Nga valley in Binh Tuy Province. Planning proceeded at a somewhat leisurely speed, and a parachute descent by the US battalions was included.

Another lesson in security was provided when shops in Bien Hoa began to stock the US parachute badge with the necessary star in the design.

The drop was cancelled, the operation brought ahead, and deployment was by helicopter and road.

Modern communications

In an attempt to foil the Vietcong spies at III CTZ headquarters, the 173rd Airborne Brigade (Separate) planned an operation in IV CTZ, and while the battalions were in that area, planned another, but delayed sending the copies of the operation order to headquarters III CTZ until the battalions had been picked up in IV CTZ and were on the way by helicopter to the new location.

The brigade could do this as it had its own support battalion and did not need to work with other units during planning its own operations.

Even so, as the helicopters with 1RAR aboard were approaching the landing zone, only minutes after III CTZ had received its copies of the operation order, a signals intercept operator with 1RAR intercepted a warning from someone in Bien Hoa to the enemy in the target area that 'the Americans are on the way!'

Marksmanship

A 1RAR patrol along the bank of the Song Be river saw one of the dream targets of jungle warfare: a happy unconcerned group of Vietcong on the far bank enjoying a bath, washing clothes and taking buckets of water back up to their camp.

The patrol commander carefully led his men into position and allocated specific targets to each, and when everyone was comfortable, with a good sight picture, said, 'Fire.'

There was one burst and all the targets fell, except the man carrying a bucket of water up the river bank. One of the Aussies said,
'I bet I can hit the bucket', and instantly every weapon fired at it.

In a few seconds all that remained in the hand of the fleeing Vietcong was the handle, and as he reached the top of the bank someone shot him.

Silence; the bodies in the water drifted downstream; nothing stirred. After a while the Aussies carefully went on; another small action was over.

If in doubt, shoot
A leave party of 1RAR arrived in Saigon and when driving down Tu Do Street towards the river front came upon a British Thames truck, riddled with bullets, tyres flat, blood stains all over the sides and on the ground around it.

Questions revealed that further down the street was an accommodation building for US troops stationed in the city, guarded by military police at the doorway, inside the usual anti-car bomb barrier of cement-filled 44-gallon drums.

Next door was the *'Baby Doll'* tailor shop. A dispute had grown between the shop owners and the city gangsters and it was decided to show the shop owners that proximity to armed US troops was no excuse to avoid paying protection money.

A grenade was lobbed into the shop doorway before opening time.

Instantly the guards at the accommodation building opened fire. Coming down the street was the Thames truck, the back filled with workers going to the docks; it was thoroughly riddled.

Speeding tail light
Each morning a member of the staff of the Australian Embassy would meet his counterpart from the British embassy and they would go for a healthy early morning run – before traffic fumes increased.

On this same morning the Aussie glimpsed what he thought was the red tail light of a speeding car zip across the intersection ahead, then many more tail lights flicked across and he realised he was looking at tracer bullets. They proceeded at a careful walk to the corner and peeped around – there was the riddled Thames truck surrounded by dead and wounded bleeding Vietnamese, who had been at the wrong place at the wrong moment when US military police felt threatened.

I think I can do
that better than
the official way

At 1RAR headquarters was a captain, graduate of RMC Duntroon, already with war service experience in South Vietnam with AATTV and US SOG. On one operation, for some reason, he thought he could strip the 9mm Owen submachine gun in a way quicker than that laid down in training procedures. He decided to try his faster method.

Unfortunately, he failed to consider the very first step in weapon cleaning: *make sure the gun is unloaded.*

Suddenly, in the middle of battalion headquarters, there was a burst of automatic fire; everyone ducked and looked around. No one was visible above ground with a weapon in hand. The captain was in the bottom of his pit, out of sight.

The Owen had fired all 28 rounds in the magazine. The burst of fire had shredded leaves in a tree directly above the battalion commander and executive officer.

It's a different Army

Soon after the CH-47 Chinook began operations, some were damaged by ground fire during a troop lift of the US 173rd Airborne Brigade, including 1RAR. A Chinook was at the side of the landing zone when the infantry of 1RAR walked past. Two US pilots were nearby and as the Aussies walked past, the senior pilot said to the junior that the CH-47 would have to be flown to Saigon for repairs.

The passing Aussies were astounded to hear the junior pilot say he would do it only if he got a DFC for the flight. In an army where medals were a rarity regardless of the events, to hear someone bargain about doing his duty was unheard of among the Australians.

You won't see us,
but we will be there

1RAR was loaned by the 173rd Airborne Brigade to the US 1st Infantry Division, and assigned to guard the division field headquarters. The Australian battalion commander explained how he would handle this task, to the disbelief of the US command. Rather than have troops standing guard around the headquarters, a comforting sight, with armoured vehicles patrolling in circles, the Australians would patrol and ambush out to mortar range and no enemy would be allowed to close in on the US headquarters.

A senior US officer declared that this would not work, and reportedly bet a case of Scotch that the enemy would be able to mortar the headquarters, if not do more.

The battalion spread out into its assigned company areas and enjoyed a successful operation, with ambushes and patrols. The headquarters was not touched. No one admits to seeing any of the Scotch.

How to disappear forever

The 1RAR Intelligence Officer and a couple of NCOs were driving in the 1RAR TAOR one day when a small USAF truck appeared driving east along the main road that ran from the town of Tan Phu to a few villages and ended in the distant bush; no one went far that way.

The truck was chased and the driver told to halt. The two occupants were a sergeant and an airman who said they were just going for a drive to look for a quiet village where they could make friends and enjoy off-duty time. They had not told anyone where they were going.

The Australian officer told them there were no such places ahead, only the border of the controlled area and beyond that enemy territory, and that other Americans had gone driving and never returned. They were advised to go back and remain in the air base and city area, and never to assume a quiet piece of the country was without potential for danger.

Cost effectiveness

There are those who like to look at statistics and observe how wars have become ever more expensive in every way. One item from the Vietnam War was the marked increase in number of small arms rounds fired that resulted in one dead enemy, and for Vietnam one figure given was 50,000 rounds for one enemy dead.

One reason for this would not be, as assumed, uncontrolled firing on full automatic, though there was that aspect. In earlier wars, rifle men trained on standard wide open firing ranges to qualify, but in action there was little that resembled a home base firing range, whether it be North Africa, Italy, France or Germany, or Korea. This resulted in the famous finding that a large percentage of riflemen did not fire in battle.

By the time of involvement in South Vietnam, firing training was more realistic and troops at least were able to fire towards an enemy even if he was not seen.

Another factor in South Vietnam was the US practice when on operations of clearing their perimeter at dusk and dawn by every man, sometimes to the extent of 100 rounds each. This expenditure added hundreds of thousands of round to the tally of all those fired, and, in the opinion of the author, resulted in the enormous figure of round fired for one enemy known to be killed.

It was sometimes disconcerting to be on a neighbouring hillside when the Americans on the next one cleared their perimeter this way.

That's who you
will take

The Australian Defence force had no intention nor desire to become involved in the war in South Vietnam, apart from small detachments of Army advisors and a RAAF DeHavilland Caribou flight. The decision to commit an infantry battalion group, then a task force, and RAAF bomber, helicopter and transport squadrons, and RAN ships, came without warning from the political offices.

Consequently there was a lack of professionalism in some subsequent deployments. The commanding officer of the Divisional Intelligence Unit in Sydney, a mixed reserve and Regular outfit, was peacefully attending to routine matters early in 1966 when his phone rang; a caller from higher headquarters in Canberra.

The caller asked for detail of those in the various sections of the unit, interrogation, air intelligence, counter-intelligence and administration who were Regular Army and medically fit for overseas service. The unit commander consulted the manning board on the wall before him, gave the details, and was stunned when his caller told him that number would be the establishment of the detachment he would command and take to South

Vietnam.

His protests that this would create an unbalanced unit, and a better establishment could be created in a few days, were ignored; action would be taken in Canberra that day to create a detachment as described. So it was, and years passed before the authorities agreed to a more useful establishment.

There are two types
of people: those who
play golf and those
who do not
When the Intelligence detachment packed up for its move to South Vietnam, one of the warrant officers put his golf clubs in with the other unit stores.

After arrival, when driving somewhere and a suitable piece of dry paddy field was found, he would stop, unpack the clubs and have some practice. Local farmers and their families were astounded to see a foreigner stop his vehicle, take out a slim steel rod, place a tiny white ball on the ground and hit it into the distance, then drive up and repeat the performance. This just could not be explained nor understood; why would any adult do such a senseless thing?

An intruder
During the Tet Offensive, when the Vietcong were in Saigon and other cities, and security of buildings was increased, an Australian living in an apartment building was awakened by the sounds of someone carefully creeping along the passageway outside. The apartment was on the second floor, easily reached by someone from the ground.

Carefully the Aussie got out of bed, pistol in hand, and crouched at the door to look along the corridor. No one was visible in the dim light but the sound of loose floor tiles, dating from French times, being stepped on continued.

The Aussie stared harder and saw a small dim shape approaching... the household cat.

Just account for every
dollar and all will be well
An Australian officer who met the requirements for a commission in peacetime operated on simple themes: obedience to rules and regulations

meant no adverse reports; what the enemy might do was beyond control; strict accounting for every dollar of government money was necessary, because inability to account for ten dollars anywhere was cause for dismissal.

When this officer arrived to command the 1ATF Intelligence detachment, and found that he was to control agents who were to be paid from a secret fund, but for payments from which no receipts could be expected, he had a simple career-protection move.

He signed for the amount of money received from his predecessor, ruled a line below, and put the book and money back into his office safe, where it all remained untouched for 12 months. When his successor arrived the agent network had been neglected for a year; no contact had been made with anyone. But no adverse finding for unauthorised expenditure could ever be made against him.

Very accurate artillery

During the fighting at Fire Support Base 'Coral' in May-June 1968, NVA night ground assaults pressed right into the 1RAR position, and close air strikes, mortars and artillery were called in and controlled. The US command welcomed these events as it meant the enemy could be subjected to the full range of firepower available, with terrible results for the attackers.

An NVA unit was pushing forward towards an Aussie fighting pit when a 155mm shell from a US battery arrived and the enemy disappeared in the blast.

Next day an Australian artillery commander was walking around the position, and had the huge crater pointed out by the Aussie Diggers, and one said,
'I don't know how you did that, sir, but it was right on time and in the right place!'

The gunner officer was as surprised as anyone else, but nodded calmly to give the impression it was all part of the normal service.

Air power

In January 1966 the 173rd Airborne Brigade deployed to IV Corps for an operation among the canals and fields there. In the 1RAR area the effect of US air power on the local population was brought home to a couple of the soldiers and officers.

Local people were terrified of any type of aircraft and hid whenever engine noise was heard. They had been too frightened to go to market because every time they set out by canoe they would be machine gunned by prowling helicopters.

Their fright was obvious, and disturbed the Aussies, but soon the brigade moved on, though the memory of the effect of modern counter-revolutionary warfare on peasants remained.

A message from
God – and profitable
The enormous volumes of fire during the fire support base battles of 1968 resulted in strings of green tracer from the VC/NVA criss-crossing with red tracer from US-Australian weapons.

One of the Aussie gunners was a confirmed betting man, and he thought the green and red indicated the club colours of the famous South Sydney rugby league club, the Rabbitohs, so placed a heavy bet on them to win the football that year. They did.

Ways around things
like regulations
The relative lack of value of local currency, the '*dong*' but commonly called by the old French title, 'piastre' or 'p', resulted in spending all of it that came into the possession of US and Australian troops.

At Bien Hoa, rifle company recreation rooms were built – at least partly! - with money taken from the bodies of Vietcong tax collectors. The Intelligence Section duly forwarded the captured documents, some of which clearly showed that the tax man had been in possession of thousands of '*dong*' the day before, with the receipts he carried in a haversack. It was deemed better to do this and so continue to receive captured items rather than cut off the flow by making trouble.

The successful platoons split the proceeds among themselves, with a share for company funds. The soldiers spent the money on their next leave, the company erected recreation areas with cement floors, windows, sawn timber walls and roof, et cetera.

One story presumably had its basis in fact, as all airlines changed procedures soon after. A platoon commander retained his share in the disposal of funds from a successful ambush, and on his next leave, went to Saigon. There he went to Air France and bought an around the world air ticket. He returned to the battalion and finished his tour of duty.

Back in Australia, he applied to the Army for a certain amount of leave to travel around the world. This was rejected. He then, allegedly, went to Air France in Sydney with his ticket and letters to and from army, pleaded being the victim of an uncaring military bureaucracy and asked to cash in his air ticket. Reportedly he left with several thousand Australian dollars.

It seems this was done more than once, because soon after all airlines announced that tickets purchased in a certain country would be redeemed in that currency only.

Later an officious staff officer at the Australian headquarters in Saigon wanted to know where all these sums of money were, because regulation 'xyz' paragraph '999' clearly stated all such monies were to be accounted for and handed in, accompanied by relevant official statements according to other rules and regulations, for return to the local government. This was casually ignored.

Road rules
In 1970 a newly arrived warrant officer checked in at a small specialist unit at Nui Dat. At the orderly room, the unit commander and a senior NCO said they were just going to collect a jeep from the mechanical engineers, who had installed a key ignition to it. To the question of where did the jeep come from, the reply was that it was stolen from the US Navy at Cat Lo, near Vung Tau.

While the other two thanked the mechanics for the job, the new arrival was to drive the jeep back to the unit. There it was, a nice grey USN jeep, with canopy fitted.

The new man climbed in and started back to the unit. By chance, there was no other traffic on the road in the Nui Dat headquarters area. The jeep driver set off on the way back, driving on the left, as usual in Australia.

Around the distant bend came a long wheel-base Landrover, nicely polished and with canopy fitted, and also with a 'star' plate on the bumper-bar: the commanding general of 1ATF – driving on the right.

The newly arrived warrant officer wondered why the brigadier was driving on the wrong side of the road, but as he considered the jeep had right of way, continued in his path. Ahead, he could see the brigadier's driver staring at him, but went on.

At the last second, the brigadier's driver swung the wheel and left the road, the brigadier's red face glaring back at the jeep, and at that instant the jeep driver realised *he* was on the wrong side of the road, and in a stolen jeep......

It was a case of pedal to the metal, as fortunately still there were no other vehicles in sight, speed around the corner before the brigadier got back out onto the road, into the unit and park behind the ablutions block out of sight, grab an NCO, to get some soldiers with a tin of green paint, take off the canopy and change the appearance of the jeep asap.

As the jeep was not Australian, the Australian military police did not pay official attention to it, though they did unofficially warn that it should never be involved in an accident; the USMP and VNMP ignored it because Australians drove it. To overcome the matter of a number plate, the Vietnamese words for 'running in' – *ra may* – were painted on the bumper bar, and so it trundled around the Australian area until 1ATF withdrew in October 1971.

The jeep *'ra may'*

The media

A wounded US officer who was not evacuated remained on duty until well enough to return to his unit in the field. He was made media liaison officer and dealt with many TV film crews and journalists. He noticed a strange herd mentality among them that never was explained or resolved, but continues to this day: somehow the group would decide in some mysterious way what the group attitude would be to a story, and how much attention, if any, it would receive.

Atrocities by the VC/NVA were almost always ignored – bombings in market places, mining of civilian buses, murders of school teachers or village officials – but any small error or act of revenge by the US forces was sought, found and publicised.

Some US media people openly stated that they came to South Vietnam to find instances of behaviour or policy failures that were damaging to the US government, and under US law were permitted to do so – 'freedom of the press'.

The point was sometimes made that if the media in World War 2 had behaved in this way, Allied progress would have been undermined to a state of collapse.

Administration
on the go
Another sign of the lack of preparedness of the Australian Defence Force for involvement in the war in Vietnam was that while units might rotate into and out of permanent barracks in Australia, most of the day to day administration work was done by locally employed typists and clerks, almost always women. The unit might have military chief clerks and pay clerks, et cetera, but few soldiers in those jobs.

This meant a heavy load on them when the unit deployed to South Vietnam. Some small units had no military clerks at all. One was the Intelligence detachment. No one knew much about clerical work.

When the first reports were required, no one knew how to create them according to correct procedures, nor the way to allocate file numbers according to content. But the reports were required 'now' at headquarters.

The problem was solved by a senior warrant officer, who created on the spot the designation for all reports that originated from the detachment for the remainder of its time in South Vietnam. He gave the first report the designation 'OBM0001', the second, 'OBM0002' and so on.

In later years the numbers were in the thousands and everyone in the 1ATF system, the US system, and the South Vietnamese, used it and referred to reports by the OBM-number.

'OBM' stood for *'Opray's Bloody Method'*.

The unforeseen result of this came long after, when all the files had to be handed to Australian Archives. There was consternation when the OBMs arrived there, as Archives could only administer files created and designated according to government rules and regulations. Archives declared they could not accept such unofficial materials. The location of them today is not known by the author.

The small animals

A saying in Asia about warfare refers to struggles in the farmyard, as *'when the buffalo fight, the small animals are trampled'*.

This was clearly understood by those in combat units, and especially so by one of the Aussies when clearing villages in Binh Tuy Province. It was a foggy morning, there was some shooting and roar of armoured personnel carriers as the Vietcong were flushed away into the bush. The Aussie came around a building and in front of the door were the family, on the ground, all looking at him, hands together submissively.

The father was in front, behind him was his wife, then the grandparents, then the children. The sight remained with the Aussie ever after – the average small farmer was unarmed and at the mercy of all the armed forces, the VC/NVA, the government, the US-Australian military, and as head of the family the man placed himself before them to meet whatever came to their door.

The black bikini

In Saigon, it was customary for some US and Australians to relax at lunch on the open roof-top areas of the various hotels used as offices, or living quarters. Most had a restaurant up there as well. A married couple from the Australian embassy, with a friend, went to the Brinks BOQ one lunch time.

They went out onto the open area and found some space to relax. The woman attracted immediate attention in a city with few European women, as she was blonde, with a good figure. The level of attention increased when she calmly pulled off the cotton shift and revealed a black bikini beneath.

She reclined on the beach towel and her husband took the bottle of sun tan cream and began to apply it, aware they were the absolute centre of attention – no other woman was present.

After her back was properly attended to, she turned over and the process began on her front, and by now there was no conversation at all on the rooftop. When the application of sun tan cream reached the upper inner thighs, there was almost a visible cloud of testosterone.

The media

At the time, the tallest building in Saigon was the Caravelle Hotel, of eight floors. Like most of the other tall buildings, on top was a bar and restaurant, offering a good view out over the surrounding plain. At night there was a constantly changing vista of flares, streams of tracer, artillery flashes, blinking anti-collision lights on aircraft, and sometimes the launch of a 122mm rocket fired from the paddies into Saigon.

During the Tet Offensive, the bar was a good vantage point to watch the fighting, the burning suburbs, the jets and helicopters and the daring forward air controllers in tiny Cessnas flying below treetop level along the river banks looking for Vietcong.

The rooftop bar was a favourite meeting place, particularly for the media. It was well-known that some journalists never went out into the field, the boondocks or 'boonies', but enlivened the public relations handouts from the Joint US Public Affairs Office (JUSPAO) with tales heard at the Caravelle from the people who did go, and sent these off to home office.

Those who did venture out on operations mostly took care to wear their muddy dirty field clothes to the Caravelle to demonstrate their daring.

Uh, well, I thought
it was one of us...

An ambush was in position on a well-used trail and the watchers waited. One began to doze off.

The slapping noise of fast-moving feet in Ho Chi Minh sandals was heard, and a Vietnamese voice saying,
'*Di duong nay, di duong nay* (go this way)'.

Safety catches were clicked off; the dozing Aussie awoke and said, in a normal voice,
'What did you say?'

There was the sound of scurrying feet, bushes rattled; silence. Glares from everyone else in the ambush.

How to change sides

The RVN had a program to 'welcome back' to the nation Vietcong or North Vietnamese of any rank, who were not treated as having committed any crime, but were debriefed and allowed back into society. This was the '*Chieu Hoi*' program, and those who rallied were '*hoi chanh*', but in the US-Free World military community they were generally called '*chieu hois*'.

Some were recruited into the RVN military, some into a US program where they were used to assist units in the field, as 'Kit Carson Scouts' and in 1ATF as 'Bushmen's Scouts'.

The VC/NVA were well aware of this surrender program and took every precaution to persuade their followers not to rally, and punished anyone found to have '*chieu hoi*' leaflets on their person.

One long-serving Vietcong had joined to continue the struggle against the imperialists that had taken the life of his father in the struggle against the French. Wounded at the Battle of Long Tan in August 1966, against D Company 6RAR, he was not fit enough afterwards for service in a combat unit and was assigned to the logistics organisation.

But life there became as hard as in any other unit, when the Australian counter-revolutionary warfare tactics and procedures took effect and the Vietcong could be ambushed at any time anywhere. One night, he and the rest of his unit were on the slopes of the Nui Dinh mountain mass west of Nui Dat, waiting for a resupply party to go to and return from Hoa Long township. They saw the tracer bullets and heard the shooting as the party was ambushed.

That was enough for the man, who crept away from the others and made his way to the road running from Baria to Nui Dat. There he waited until an Australian vehicle came along.

One did, and he waved it down and said, 'Nui Dat.' The Aussie driver of the Land-rover jerked his thumb towards the back and told the Vietnamese to climb in, which he did, and settled among the unit laundry that was collected.

At the gate into the Nui Dat base, the Vietcong was told to get out of the vehicle, did so, and he waited while the soldier on duty telephoned the Intelligence detachment to come and collect a local with no pass.

This they did. This indicates the scale of the defeat inflicted on the VC/NVA by late 1970, and the casual attitude of drivers in the 1ATF area towards itinerant locals.

What the hell happened?

In the dry season of 1970-71, a North Vietnamese was the hapless victim of the technical superiority of the enemy. He was in a Vietcong unit in the Long Hai mountain range east of Vung Tau, fishing in one of the numerous bomb craters on the eastern side of the range.

A bush-fire was burning on the slopes. Passing overhead were two RAAF armed helicopters, 'Bushrangers', and from one of them someone saw our innocent fisherman. It was decided to attack, and by reference to the bush-fire, the exact location could be identified and both helicopters able to dive on a firing pass without needing to circle, which often was a definite warning for anyone below.

On the western side of the range was the US Special Forces B-57 camp, where a Huey was waiting, but the crew had been listening to the RAAF conversation as they prepared to attack.

The Huey lifted off from B-57 as the attack went in, the 'Bushrangers' fired their rockets, they hit all around the hapless fisherman with a tremendous roar, and raised a cloud of smoke, dust and stone chips, there was another roar and great wind and turbulence as the B-57 Huey arrived, the shocked NVA was picked up and before he knew what had happened he was on the ground at B-57, among a mass of Americans.

1ATF was asked to send an interrogation team, which it did. The NVA had a sad tale to relate. He had been drafted into the military, as was every other healthy male, trained and sent to liberate South Vietnam. Along the way the infiltration group was bombed by B-52s and fighter jets, bombarded by artillery, attacked by jungle pests, afflicted by diseases, and gradually numbers shrank. After arrival in the South, this intensified and numbers shrank again as men were provided to units in the areas they passed through. By the time the group arrived in the 1ATF area only a few were left and the man and one other were allocated to the Vietcong unit in the Long Hai mountains.

There, the age-old enmity between North and South was strongly in evidence, and the two NVA were given all the menial jobs, such as cleaning, doing guard duty, carrying water, digging latrines and similar. His friend was killed and he was the only NVA with a bunch of Southerners. Then he was sent to catch fish in the bomb crater....

The AK47
The AK-47 became famous in the Vietnam War, because of its simplicity of construction and ability to fire a 30-round magazine of 7.62mm calibre on automatic.

The weapon was named for the 'inventor', Kalashnikov, who engaged in a typical piece of Soviet lying about the development of the weapon. Allegedly, Kalashnikov was a patriotic veteran of the WW2 campaigns on the Eastern Front who became worried that the USSR did not have weapons capable of good frontline service in the conditions he experienced. Following from this, he allegedly set about solving this problem as a patriot. The AK-47 was the result, and though he retired as a general, with all the prestige and pension entitlements that went with it, he complained that he never received any royalties from the production and sale of the weapon.

Consider the circumstances in which Kalashnikov allegedly developed the AK-47. At the end of World War 2 in 1945, with the defeat of Nazi Germany, Russia, Poland, the Ukraine, and all the other countries occupied by the Soviets, were in ruins. Open plundering took place of factories and towns and cities by Soviet forces, to ship back to Russia every machine capable of production.

To believe Kalashnikov, one would have to believe that, as a Soviet citizen, he was able to acquire for his personal use the machine tools and lathes, the facilities for making the weapon parts and ammunition in all stages of development, shooting ranges, chemicals for development of the ammunition propellant, technical support for calculations regarding metallurgy, access to relevant offices to assist in calculations on muzzle velocity, and every other detail.

Such personal freedom did not exist in totalitarian Communist societies, and his first mortal sin would have been to imply that the Party had failed to provide adequate weapons. He would have been taken by the security police, tried and shot at the beginning of his alleged efforts.

Kalashnikov was a servant of the regime from start to finish and the story of the enthusiastic individual working for the motherland is a lie.

I'll take the mail
with me
A US major disappeared on one operation walking alone between brigade headquarters and one of the battalions. It was a distance of less than 800 yards or metres, and he volunteered to take the battalion mail with him. When he did not return, radio traffic revealed he had not arrived at the battalion. A search party found his boot prints, then a number of prints made by the 'Ho Chi Minh' sandals worn by the VC, and his prints eventually were overtaken by those from the sandals, and both sets went into the jungle and no more tracking could be done. The major was never heard of again.

5.56mm ammunition
The Aussies were impressed by the wide range of weapons available to the US forces to deliver firepower to any given location.

The 5.56mm AR15, later M16, was a welcome replacement for the worn-out Australian 9mm Owen machine carbine, still in use after World War 2. The AR15 was light, modern, with black plastic, had a handy bipod to keep it up out of the dirt, and a lot of 5.56mm ammunition could be carried. The first supplies of 5.56 were from Olin-Mathieson.

The reputation of the AR15 was impressive and wounds inflicted were said to be fatal wherever inflicted.

Then problems began to be experienced. The rifle jammed when fired on single shot or on automatic, and sometimes the plastic stock split when water found its way inside, could not be compressed and recoil ruptured the stock. Some people handed them back and took the solid and working 7.62mm SLR.

A mass of complaints filtered back to higher US headquarters, but these were brushed aside by people well back in the system. The reply to complaints was that the soldiers were not cleaning or maintaining their AR15 or M16 correctly.

In the first big battle fought by the US 1st Air Cavalry Division at the Ia Drang, in November 1965, there were many failures of the M16. At least one rifle company in 1/7th Cavalry had to re-organise into three-man teams, of which one man with a cleaning rod kept the other two supplied with working rifles – cartridge cases would jam in the breech and could only be forced out by pressure down the barrel with a cleaning rod.

The authorities refused to accept that any item of issued US equipment was faulty.

At long last an investigation showed the cause, created by the arrogant whiz kids of McNamara's Defense Department, who did not let the minor matter of lack of practical experience in military affairs hold them back.

When the AR15/M16 was designed by Gene Stoner, he also specified the ammunition propellant. But in Washington DC someone knew better and a large quantity of artillery propellant in, reportedly, a warehouse in Kansas, was used for 5.56mm rifle ammunition. This unsuitable alteration to the weapon design resulted in hundreds or thousands of jammed rifles, most in action, at the worst possible moment.

Is everyone here?
1RAR and the battalions of the 173rd Airborne Brigade were flying from Vo Dat south to Xuan Loc, in CH-47 Chinooks. One Chinook lost power and dropped from the formation, but was able to land safely in a clearing. The 1RAR infantry aboard spread out around the helicopter while the crew attended to the problem. When it was fixed all climbed aboard as the engines revved and the aircraft took off to continue the flight.

The 1RAR platoon sergeant counted those aboard.. oops, seem to be missing a few; counted again… yes; some have been left behind!

A quick radio message to Xuan Loc resulted in Huey gunships speeding to the location, already known from the messages sent as the Chinook descended.

The gunships returned with the hapless Aussies, and reported they had no trouble finding them. The small team was that of the Assistant Quarter-Master, who had the radio and smoke grenades used for bringing in helicopter re-supplies, and there was a large smoke cloud rising from the location.

Cultural differences – 3

The impression of sheer power in the overwhelming US presence at Bien Hoa gripped everyone in the 1RAR Group. Jet fighters of many types arrived and departed, transports, reconnaissance aircraft including the secret U-2 flew past, and formations of forty or fifty Bell UH-1D Hueys were commonplace.

For anyone in the tiny Australian Defence Force, scattered around a continent as large as the USA to have injections of federal funds available to those communities, and to provide employment for the necessary thousands of public servants, here was serious military force.

Just how impressive was attention to detail in providing for the troops was demonstrated in several ways, each a marked contrast to the niggardly attitude of the Australian government. Every day a huge USAF C-124 Globemaster four-engine propellor driven transport would arrive at Bien Hoa from the north-east, join the circuit and land. Later it would take-off and fly away to the north-east.

One of the Aussies asked about this regular arrival and departure and was astounded to be told the aircraft flew in daily from Okinawa with the fresh fruit and vegetables for the 173rd Airborne Brigade.

Hepatitis rolls

One thing the Vietnamese did learn from the French was how to bake bread. These rolls, or baguettes, were available in most places and street stalls sold them filled with a variety of food types, including items from the black market or stolen from US bases. This might include ham that should have been kept refrigerated until the tin was opened.

Given the local lack of Western hygiene in growing vegetables or in food preparation, though many Aussies enjoyed these rolls, they were commonly called 'hepatitis rolls' because of the danger of illness. No one seemed to worry about it.

1ATF vehicle numbers

The Vietnamese were typical Asian drivers – lacking skill and judgement, and accidents were frequent. Some of the more thoughtful noted the number plates of Australian vehicles, and, after an accident, complained that the Australian driver of 'xxx-xxx' vehicle was at fault, backed by friends, witnesses and a lawyer.

Hapless Aussie drivers then were required to explain this situation, made worse by the extra factor of having disobeyed an Australian order and left the scene of an accident before Military Police arrived. However, investigation showed that sometimes the vehicle had been nowhere near Vung Tau, Baria or other accident location and had not left the 1ATF base or 1ALSG base that day.

Just another attempt to exploit the rich foreigners.

A handy design feature

The standard issue steel trunk for Australian soldiers going overseas, in the days of troop ships, was termed a 'trunk, cabin, metal' in the usual Service way of describing things.

These were sturdy things, secured by a hasp and lock, with a good amount of space below and on top was a tray with two sections, for underwear and similar.

A senior warrant officer arrived in a unit as a continuation of service already in-country with another Australian unit, where he had been involved in certain financial aspects of unit procedures. Due to his rank and position, he was allocated a batman, a bit of a bushman from civilian life.

Word soon got around that the warrant officer's metal trunk had the top tray containing only two things: US dollars and local currency. Whenever the batman had a day on leave, he did not use his own money, but took enough from both parts of the tray.

Later, back in Australia, the warrant officer was charged and court-martialled with infringements of the regulations, and was found guilty, sentenced to be reduced to the rank of lance-corporal and discharged. However, there were a lot of wily old foxes in that level of rank, and he calmly allowed proceedings to go on to their conclusion, then pointed out that the charges laid were incorrect, which they were found to be, the correct charges should have been so-and-so, and that double jeopardy meant he could not be charged twice, so he must be allowed to retain his rank and pension rights, but he now requested discharge.

Vietcong on leave
in Vung Tau
A common myth was that the Vietcong also went to Vung Tau on leave, and could be seen strolling along in their black pyjamas, with little Vietcong lapel badges. This was untrue.

The Vietnamese seen walking along the beach or in town were at the government Revolutionary Development Cadre School (RDC) based on the peninsula north of Vung Tau. They were part of a government program to train men and women to go into country areas, dress modestly like the locals, live with them, share their experiences, and offer advice on agriculture, hygiene, civic duties and similar. The RDC badge was small and similar at first glance to a Vietcong badge.

The Vietcong did not allow much leave, partly to retain control over people, partly to prevent them being persuaded by family to 'rally', and partly because they did not have a leave component in their system of service. Some people rallied because of this.

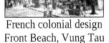
French colonial design
Front Beach, Vung Tau

Aussies on leave
in Vung Tau
The Australian leave centre was established in Vung Tau. A cartoon listed the local slang and vocabulary.

Cheap Charlie   (miserly)
Uc-dai-loi bar-me-lum (sexually voracious)
I love you too much
I love you beaucoup

Give me twenty p	
Buy me one tea	
Bar-me-ba	('33' brand beer)
You have Salem?	(menthol cigarette of the time)
The five-ways	(a street junction)
You dinky-dao	(insane, from *dien ky dau*)
Choi oi	(gosh!)
FIGMO	(finally I got my orders [to return to the USA])
Back beach	(the ocean beach)
Front beach	(the city waterfront, for the Vietnamese)
Cowboy	Vietnamese youth, young crooks
That's a ten-two-three	Military police code for an event
It's a ten-thirty-three	ditto
It's twenty-two hundred	curfew time

The media

This might be a myth, but was related with approval in 1970, with some disappointment at the ending

.

Under MACV policy, media representatives were to be given seats on any form of transport going to anywhere the media desired, with the priority equal to anyone of the rank of major or equivalent.

A TV crew arrived at the airfield and asked for seats on a helicopter going to fire support base 'X'. A CH-47 Chinook was available, so the TV crew carried all their gear aboard, the only passengers. They noticed the surly looks from the load-master and door gunner, but settled in and the Chinook took off.

One of the TV men was worried by the unfriendly looks from the two men, and that they seemed to be talking to the pilots. Then both crewmen smiled and turned their attention to outside the Chinook.

As the Chinook began to descend to their destination the two crewmen, smiling, gestured to the TV crew that they would land very soon. The TV crew man wondered what had caused the change in attitude.

The Chinook landed in the usual cloud of dust, the rear ramp dropped and the smiling cabin crew gestured to the TV crew to leave. The man who wondered at the change looked out and saw, through the dust, that the fire support base was abandoned and empty, and realised what had been intended – to leave them somewhere out in the bush, and, if questioned, shrug and say that it was where the TV crew wanted to go.

He quickly waved the others back, and to sit down and do up seat-belts. As the Chinook could not sit on the ground for long, it soon took off and delivered the crew to where they had requested, but the incident left no doubt about how the media was regarded by some in the military.

How did a truck get there?
The Australian Army Aviation unit at 1ATF flew daily low-level reconnaissance flights over the area, usually with an observer aboard, often from the air intelligence section of the Intelligence detachment.

On one flight early in the morning, the sun's rays were at just the right angle to shine through the trees and reflect off something below. The aircraft circled and suddenly the image came into focus – down there was a truck windscreen and the distinctive long sloping bonnet of a truck.

Try as they might, the crew could not see any sign of an access route to the spot for a truck, quite obviously a two-and-a-half tonner. It was known that the Vietcong had trucks and the NVA used hundreds along the Ho Chi Minh Trail further north, the 'Molotova' Russian copy of the famous US vehicle. How one would be this far south was a puzzle, and no other sign of how it was driven there could be seen.

The site was recorded and at 1ATF it was decided to send a helicopter, from which a man would descend on the winch and investigate. This was done, and the intrepid investigator found that what was there was not a truck, but the front of a North American F-100 Super Sabre jet fighter, which had a distinctive long sloping nose and slanted front canopy, that, from a distance, through the tree canopy, resembled a truck.

In the cockpit were the remains of the pilot. Investigation showed that the F-100 had crashed during a bombing attack some distance away months earlier, in full view of the Australian ground forces, and the recovery had resulted officially in the pilot's remains being recovered and returned to the USA for burial. The forward part of the fuselage and cockpit had been flung far ahead of the impact site. What was found in the cockpit there was handed to the USAF and quietly disposed of.

Graffiti 1970
The US military system by 1970 was deeply troubled by racial problems, drugs, and lack of morale and enthusiasm resulting from lack of significant progress in achieving a victory – unlike in the World Wars – and the obvious lack of success in the 'peace talks'. A piece of graffiti summed up the attitude of many US soldiers:

> *We are the unlucky*
> *Led by the unqualified*
> *Doing the unnecessary*
> *For the ungrateful*

For the ungrateful
Despite all the political propaganda phrases about the long history of Vietnam and defending democracy, there were few illusions among the US-Free World military forces about the degree of corruption in the South Vietnamese government, at all levels.

Military officers were 'appointed' as mayors and chiefs of districts and provinces, but these offices were bought at the highest levels and the purchase price had to be recouped for the investors.

Huge sums were to be made on the black market, and shipments of US goods sent to assist in commercial development, as aid projects, were plundered by the local officers in authority.

The US-Australian military police soon learned that the South Vietnamese police would not dare to operate against bars and hotels, because they knew who were the generals who owned those businesses.

After the failure of a series of raids it became known that the chief of customs at Vung Tau was one of the main people in the black market.

The Grand Hotel, Vung tau, was the biggest and best known, and it was the desire of the military police to successfully raid it, to show all the smaller outfits that no one was immune. Eventually this was done, and a huge supply of black market material was found, but it was all done in a friendly way, as the hotel owner had been a lieutenant in army service with President Nguyen Van Thieu.

What never was found was the main cache of US beer that supplied the bars in the Grand.

The people sniffer
The never-ending search for ways to locate the VC/NVA so firepower could be delivered to that location resulted in many attempts to use technology to conquer terrain and foliage.

One was the Airborne Personnel Detector, commonly called the 'people sniffer'. This was a machine carried by helicopter or light aircraft low over forest and jungle, that had the air sampled through a flexible tube and brought to a machine that detected ammonia and gave a reading on a dial.

The idea was to gain an indication of concentrations as an aid to Intelligence collection programs. The device worked best in dry weather soon after sunrise, before wind or breeze dispersed the concentration. Wet weather, bush fires and smoke from nearby villages made use of the device unsuccessful.

The RAAF used one Huey to fly a 'ploughing' pattern back and forth over the selected area, nominated by 1ATF, with a second Huey higher to the rear as guide and controller to keep the first aircraft on track, with two armed Hueys along for protection and reaction.

It was not unknown for the RAAF to arbitrarily change the search area to somewhere safe and with no threat of ground fire so that a visiting senior officer could fly an operational sortie and so be eligible for the campaign medal. 1ATF protests were ignored – the RAAF had the helicopters. (See 'Vengeance' below.)

Australian Army Aviation used a Pilatus Porter to do the 'ploughing' flight with another as guide. There were no Army gunships.

But all this was only one way to collect information, and was a fast way to check an area, given other factors applied.

The Vietcong had agents everywhere in the government system, so the secret of the device did not last long. In addition, US forces flying 'sniffer' missions routinely attacked locations with a high reading, about as useful as artillery H&I – 'maybe there is someone there'. The VC found that colonies of monkeys had been strafed and no great powers of deduction were needed to arrive at the conclusion of what caused these attacks. So precautions were taken in all jungle camps to conceal or disperse odours from cooking and human waste.

*We can't get rid
of this stuff* .
Despite the never-ending thirst for beer, there was one brand that was unpopular with everyone concerned, whether for legal sale or on the black market. The US PX and camp entertainment systems quite legally sought and bought Australian beer. In later years uninformed historians in Australia looked at the quantity of beer shipped from Australia to South Vietnam and assumed the Aussie soldiers were drinking it. In reality they consumed only a fraction – all the rest went to genuine commercial customers. Most soldiers were in the field for long times and no beer was supplied out there.

To spread the benefits, the Australian canteen services had to buy equally from Australian breweries. However, there was one brand of Aussie beer, from West Australia, that no one would drink, even West Aussies. The Americans would not have it, and neither would anyone else. Pallets of this stuff piled up in tents at Nui Dat. When the Aussies left, a huge hole was dug and the undrinkable shoved into it, where it remains.

Nuoc Mam
Nuoc mam was the Vietnamese fish sauce enjoyed by the local people with every meal. There were variations in taste according to location of production, and some was very highly regarded.

It is made by placing layers of fish and salt in a container that is sealed, and allowed to stand. The natural process completely dissolves the fish and the end product is very nourishing. Westerners found the odour very strong – understandably!

The chemical reaction of *nuoc mam* with the US-supplied government issued aluminium water bottle eventually ate away the bottle, and was one reason why plastic water bottles were provided for service in South Vietnam.

The whaler

Vung Tau is on the southern tip of the peninsula of that name, and it became a large air and naval base for Vietnamese, US and Australian activities. To the north-east, across a wide bay with excellent beaches, on the tip of the mainland was the coastal resort town of Long Hai. Here were many attractive structures built in the French colonial time, of that comfortable tropical design. Long Hai was where wealthy Saigonese enjoyed their holidays, and crews of helicopters passing spoke of the good-looking women in bikinis often seen there.

This encouraged two US Navy junior ranks to take a Boston whaler, some cold drinks and high hopes of meeting well-filled bikinis, across the bay to the Long Hai area.

They had not done enough preparation, because the Saigonese were there when there were holidays, and on this day there were no people on vacation. The two adventurers went from place to place along the coast, without finding girls, but did attract the attention of the Vietcong, who assumed this was a spying mission.

The destination of the whaler was easy to predict, and at one place our two voyagers were captured and taken to a cave. The Vietcong were overjoyed to have two spies, and left one man to guard them while all the others rushed off to report to higher headquarters. The US sailors now realised their predicament.

What with all the excitement, the lone guard became tired and went to sleep. The Americans knew this would be their only opportunity, hit the guard with a rock, ran out of the cave and kept on going to a South Vietnamese defence post.

Their administrative and disciplinary problems in the US system were just beginning, but the captured whaler became the centre of attention. Several different units decided they could make good use of a whaler, and planned to recapture it.

An Australian operation on the eastern side of the Long Hais was in progress, with M113 armoured personnel carriers and infantry. Word arrived about the whaler, and it was decided at a low level of command to take some M113s to the reported location, take back the whaler, and enjoy its use thereafter. No one knew how big a whaler is, and thought the boat in question was about the size of a dinghy, that could be tossed aboard an M113.

At Vung Tau itself, the Vietnamese Navy (VNN) Junk Force, with US naval advisors, also decided to take the whaler, gathered a small fleet of motorised junks, a motor gun boat, and set off. Quickly invited along, and happy to accept, was a newly arrived RAN Clearance Diving Team, CDT3.

By the fortunes of war, the M113s and naval force arrived at the same time, but oblivious of each other's presence. The Vietcong, disappointed about the escape of the two prisoners, occupied themselves shooting from the Long Hai hills at the enemy.

The Junk Force raiders splashed ashore, but one of the RAN divers regretted his decision to take along his 9mm F1 machine carbine, which somehow came apart in his hands in the surf, and he was left with the useless stock and receiver. The barrel and bolt were in the water somewhere.

The M113 crews were busily firing inland and looking for this small boat, when they were amazed to find people in black clothes – dressed like the Vietcong – rushing past from the sea, and running about searching for the boat. A couple of the divers thought it would be a good idea to be near the M113s, and learned a lesson long known to infantry – keep away from big armoured vehicles, because the enemy shoot at them with everything they have.

Meanwhile, the weather had worsened and the junks were driven ashore, so far up the beach that they could not be towed off by the gun boat, which itself managed to have its propellor fouled by a cable. It drifted off-shore, under fire from the Vietcong, who raked it with a machinegun, forcing the crew to seek cover behind the small superstructure.

Meanwhile, the senior Australian armour officer had been airborne over the land-ward operation and returned to Nui Dat to refuel. As he flew back south, along the mountain range, he became aware something was happening, saw Vietcong below firing out to sea, and was amazed to find a small fleet of ships off-shore and a battle in progress on the beach, where nothing had been happening when he was there earlier.

It became obvious that a disaster was brewing. The junks were ashore, with no way off the beach, the gun boat had its own problems, the whaler was found but was far too big to just throw on top of a M113 and be driven away, so it was blown up, and all the crews of the Junk Force, USN advisors, and CDT3, had to be moved out of the battle area. Only the M113s were available – a fortuitous aspect.

The term 'packed like sardines' applied as the Australian infantry with the M113s, the Junk Force, advisors and CDT3 squeezed inside, under fire. The force set off along the beach, and one of the M113 crews thought it looked magnificent, speeding armoured vehicles racing along with huge rooster tails of spray behind them.

Then one of the M113s hit a rock at full speed. The vehicle surged up and became stuck at an angle, the back roof hatch was open and waves began to flow inside, but no one could get out because the Vietcong brought every weapon to bear on this excellent target. One of the divers thought drowning was imminent.

But another M113 crewman, under fire, attached a tow-rope to the stuck vehicle and it was pulled free, then the gallop up the beach resumed.

Peace returned to the beach. But in the excitement, two people had been left behind – the senior US advisor and the VNN commander of the Junk Force. They realised their futures were not of the best. The gunboat had gone, the M113s had gone; Vietcong would be on the beach soon to inspect the abandoned junks.

From out of the dusk, apparently oblivious to recent events, a man on a motorcycle appeared driving along the beach road. The two officers realised that this was their only chance of escape, so 'persuaded' the man to have his motorbike commandeered, to be collected later at a government office in Baria, and the two very lucky officers set off north along the road.

The Vietcong congratulated themselves on a great day. They had caught spies, driven off a naval landing and captured two junks, driven off an armoured assault and chased the whole force away up the beach. It was the stuff of legends.

A return visit by the USN-VNN later found the junks looted, and it was not possible to recover them, so they were burned on the spot.

It all worked for once, beautifully

In late February 1966, 1RAR was assigned to protect a US Engineer unit building a road well to the north of Bien Hoa. The usual Australian practice had rifle companies ranging far and wide around the area. A series of small contacts occurred and after a few days a trend was recognised.

The Vietcong were probing and making reconnaissance before a big attack on the engineers. The 1RAR commander and senior officers informed the US command and preparations began to meet the attack. Tanks and infantry arrived to defence the engineers, with 1RAR positioned to one side.

A series of small ambush actions were fought in the night, as the Vietcong attackers were brought across country to the assembly areas and the attack went in. The tanks, infantry, engineers and Aussies fired; Vietcong on the tanks were hosed off with machine guns; the bush and shrubs were levelled.

Dawn revealed a scene of slaughter. Dead enemy littered the ground. This was the result of a major weakness in the enemy command and control system. Once an operation was decided upon, units alerted, and approach marches begun, there was no effective way of changing the plan.

The Vietcong tactic of holding assault forces well away from the objective, then making a fast approach, relied on the enemy doing nothing during that time, measured in hours. This was their 'three fast, one slow' procedure: fast approach, fast assault, fast withdrawal, slow preparation. It worked well against static positions occupied by government units, but not against the US-Australian force.

Three assault battalions had covered 25 km on the approach, then, regardless of the flurry of ambushes, dutifully were brought to the attack position.

150 enemy dead were found. Using a cautious but reliable figure from battles over the years, for every death there usually are three or four wounded, so the three battalions would have had about 600 casualties in all, at a minimum.

This was the result of good work by the Intelligence Officer 1RAR, who received no official recognition for his work in battlefield Intelligence.

How do you tell
a veteran?

The US forces were good at identifying trends and differences. It was noticed that in South Vietnam there was a higher frequency of head wounds than in previous conflicts.

Investigation showed that soldiers were bleaching their canvas helmet cover, that was supplied with a camouflage pattern, to indicate to newer arrivals that the man had been so long in South Vietnam that the sun had bleached the colour from the canvas, and the wearer was an old hand in-theatre.

Other men tucked into the elastic band supplied to hold twigs and leaves in place on the helmet their white mite- and mosquito-repellent bottles, or cigarettes, which often were the distinctive bright red of the well-known tobacco brands.

All this made easy targeting for the Vietcong.

Oh, what a beautiful
morning…

An Australian cavalry officer was detached as liaison to the ARVN headquarters at Tan Uyen, on the scenic Dong Nai River. All was quiet and he thought he would go down to the river for a wash and contemplative shave.

Dressed only in a towel, carrying his toilet gear, and wearing shower shoes, or flip-flops, he strolled down to the water's edge, had a wash and lathered up.

He noticed some splashes out on the water, and that the splashes were coming closer to him. A moment of puzzlement at this phenomenon and then realisation: someone out there was shooting at him!

As he later related, try running up a river bank in shower shoes, towel flapping, under fire….

The Warbies

West of the 1ATF base at Nui Dat was a large clump of mountains, the Nui

Dinh massif. A popular US song of the time was '*Wolverton Mountain*', where a grumpy old mountain man guarded his daughter and young men were advised to keep away.

This was applied to the Nui Dinhs, and over time '*Wolverton*' became corrupted to '*Warburton*', then to '*Warby*' and around 1ATF troops referred to '*the Warbys*'.

You'll have to go
and find them

Australian civilians of many types and with many skills went to South Vietnam to seek employment in local businesses, especially those with a US head office, as 'third country nationals' in the huge range of commercial enterprises. These people travelled on Australian passports and were required to register with the Australian embassy, and give details of their employer and residence.

When the Tet Offensive broke, no one knew where all these Aussies were, or if they were OK, had been forced out of accommodation because of fighting, or were captured by the enemy.

A corporal linguist at the Australian headquarters in Saigon was called in, given a list of names and addresses, and told to find all those people, advise them to check in with the embassy, and be prepared to depart South Vietnam if the situation worsened.

This duty meant using a map of Saigon, keeping up with the latest announcements of success by the VC/NVA, and carefully investigating alleyways, lanes and small streets throughout the over-crowded city.

The corporal later said it was almost unbelievable where some of these Aussies were living, but all were found successfully.

One wealthy Aussie businessman and long-time resident had done well by buying duck feathers, paid his workers well and treated them well, but neither he nor his sister had notified the embassy of her presence. When fires in the area of the feather warehouse alarmed him, as his sister was there, the businessman went there, was turned back by VC guards, but thought he could outwit them and tried to bypass them. He was captured, moved out of Saigon and held for some weeks before release.

Rehabilitation

During an action an Aussie platoon sergeant received much of the force of the explosion of an RPG round. He had a leg blown off, an eye destroyed, and shrapnel wounds. He was evacuated by RAAF helicopter, then returned to Australia. He found that the government office concerned would provide him with a wheel-chair and walking stick, but he personally investigated what was available and from Canada had supplied a device with artificial leg that allowed him some mobility on his 'feet'. He also retrained in clerical duties and continued his Army service.

In later years the effects of the shrapnel wounds expanded to the degree that he could no longer perform clerical work, even as a supervisor, so requested discharge. As part of the procedure, he enquired about the pension he expected, as a result of his wounds and inability to work to support himself.

The response was classic unfeeling bureaucracy: As he had rehabilitated himself as a clerk, he would not be entitled to anything from the government.

A veterans' organisation – RDFWA, not the RSL – took up his case and had the matter rectified. The sergeant died a few years later.

Rehabilitation - extra

In the course of the investigation into the above case by RDFWA, it was found that the RAAF pilot who flew the evacuation had looked back as the sergeant was loaded aboard, and the sight of the casualty, the reddened head and arms bandages, other blood-soaked bandages flapping in the wind, then a severed leg tossed aboard, so affected the RAAF officer that he became unable to fly, was discharged and had been a Totally & Permanently Incapacitated (TPI) veteran on the full range of government benefits for years.

Dinner guests

Surrendered or captured Vietcong sometimes were released by the South Vietnamese for interrogations by 1ATF at the Nui Dat base. They were accommodated in the tents of the Intelligence detachment, told not to leave there, did so, and did not constitute a security threat. They were happy to be out of danger, well fed, clothed, with showers and even cold drinks.

For meals they were taken to the HQ 1ATF Other Ranks dining building, and shown how to use a knife and fork by the Intelligence soldiers.

Some of the 1ATF headquarters people were startled to see former enemy walking along to meals, but adapted to the situation as just another strange aspect of the war.

One of the Intelligence corporals never trusted these former enemy and always slept with a 9mm Browning pistol under his pillow. One night, in the dark, he was woken by a person standing at his bedside muttering in Vietnamese... out came the pistol and a call for one of the linguists.

The Vietnamese had noted that this corporal was the chap in charge of that room where cases of C Rations were stacked, and who handed out the contents... and the Vietnamese was hungry again.

The personal weapon
An untold aspect of the Australian effort in Phuoc Tuy Province was the responsibility placed on very junior soldiers in the Intelligence detachment tasked to travel around the area and collect information from friendly offices and informants. The Australian table of organisation did not allow for enough vehicles for this activity, and the economy-minded people in the transport office often said no vehicles were available.

One young corporal simply used local public transport and caught the province bus outside Nui Dat, then smaller buses to travel around his assigned area.

One day a snap weapons check was done at the Intelligence detachment and weapon numbers checked against the identity of the person issued with a particular weapon.

The quarter-master corporal asked the young traveller for his pistol, to check the number. Everyone was amazed when he opened his holster and produced a water pistol, with the calm explanation that he knew he was vulnerable during all his travels, and that if the Vietcong wanted to take him at any time they could, so he left his pistol locked away at one of the distant outposts and carried a water pistol.

'I'll get a few squirts off at them,' he finished.

Cultural differences
– 4

One day at Bien Hoa, in the 1RAR position band music could be heard in the distance, and over there at the US artillery location was a parade, with troops in formation, flags flying, the band, and the usual small group of senior officers.

Later one of the US gunners was at 1RAR and was asked about the parade, and was it the regimental birthday or similar. The reply surprised the Aussie – it was for the award of medals.

Further questions revealed the very different policy of the US forces for awarding medals. The artillery unit had people receive medals on the basis of Vietcong killed by artillery, but based on statistics from World War 2.

The Aussies were stunned, as most of the artillery had been fired into the jungle on Harassing and Interdiction (H&I) missions, that is, at locations where it was deduced enemy might be at the very moment and not on any firm knowledge. Up to that time, there had been very few operations where artillery was called in on enemy opposing the infantry.

At this time, Australian policy was that a single campaign medal and ribbon would be issued for service in a war zone, and it was to be the British General Service Medal with a clasp 'South Vietnam', until reality was accepted and an Australian medal was created – the first by any Australian government.

Trumped

Two Australian Army units are entitled to wear the emblem of the US Presidential Unit Citation (PUC) – 3RAR for the Battle of Kapyong, Korea, April 1951, and D Company 6RAR for the Battle of Long Tan, South Vietnam, August 1966. Veterans of the battles are entitled to wear the emblem for the rest of their military service, regardless of the unit they might be in, and other people wear the emblem only while posted to the unit.

In the early 1970s 3RAR was located at Woodside in South Australia. Also there was an Air Defence Regiment and the Army Intelligence Centre.

The self-important Regimental Sergeant Major (RSM) of 3RAR walked up to a group of Intelligence people and noticed one officer wearing the PUC. In his best RSM's official voice, to remind all there of his presence, he asked why the officer was wearing the PUC.

The quiet reply was, 'I commanded 10 Platoon at Long Tan.' Silence.

Stiff upper lip –
trembling knees
During a night ambush the Vietcong survivors fled when it was sprung, some running past the ambushers. One Aussie had a speeding figure leap over him and disappear in the darkness. The Aussie could hear a strange rustling noise in the leaves close by, and carefully looked around, then realised the noise was from his knees shaking and rustling leaves there.

Daily civilian life
and its dangers
A civilian Australian surgical team worked at the Bien Hoa hospital during the time 1RAR was posted there. The battalion commander agreed to allow his two linguists to assist the team whenever the battalion was not on operations.

The experience of the linguists confirmed their prejudices. The Aussie surgeons and nursing sisters worked all day as required by the work-load, but the Vietnamese arrived whenever it suited them, observed siesta and took frequent smoking and chatting breaks.

Many of the patients suffered from injuries acquired by reckless driving, and a typical injury was a wound to the heel from the pedals on the Lambretta motorcycle.

Another horrific but common injury was burns resulting from using petrol in the Primus-type stove. As most Vietnamese kitchens did not have benches as in the West, the cook squatted on the floor at the stove. When the stove flared, the burst of fire hit the person on the body, inner thighs and groin. The result can be imagined easily.

There were relatively few injuries from military operations at this time, but once a VNAF Northrop F5 fighter loaded with napalm crashed on take-off and went into a village, with terrible results.

The road race
Towards the end of the Australian involvement in South Vietnam, the main

road from the centre of the province out eastwards to Xuyen Moc was improved, a great benefit to commerce and trade. It was decided to have a foot race to celebrate and to demonstrate to the enemy that good things were happening despite their desire to wreak damage.

Runners from the US forces, Australians, New Zealanders, South Koreans, and South Vietnamese arrived at the starting place, lined up, and began. At the finish line in Xuyen Moc the province chief, senior provincial officers and their counterparts from the allied forces, with many civilians, waited to celebrate the end of the race.

There was polite surprise, but local pride, when the runners appeared after a run of some 20 kilometres, and in the lead was a neatly dressed Vietnamese. Behind him came the Aussies, Yanks, Kiwis and the rest.

There were trophies for first, second and third. At the dais the province chief proudly shook the hand of the winning Vietnamese and handed him the first prize cup, but one of the staff officers stepped forward and whispered in the chief's ear.

The chief listened, looked at the winner and asked a question; the answer was a nod.

The chief took out his pistol and shot the winner, the body was dragged away, some blood wiped off the cup and it was presented with a smile to the new first place winner, formerly second place getter.

The chief had just been told the Vietnamese winner had ridden all the way to Xuyen Moc on a motor bike, then dismounted to finish in great style.

Navigating

A common sight in the Australian outback is the wind-pump, a large wind-driven propellor that pumps water whenever the wind blows. As part of the Australian aid program in Phuoc Tuy, these wind pumps, with a raised water tank, were installed in all the local villages. The name of the village was painted on the tank in large letters, for the assistance of troops patrolling, and for those in the category of 'the most dangerous thing in the Army is a second lieutenant with a map.'

Psyops

In all modern wars the use of psychological operations has been encouraged and given employment to thousands of men and women, all seeking that magical combination of words and information that will persuade the enemy to surrender, hopefully in mass.

That this rarely happens is due to many factors, chief among them that unless people are in very desperate circumstances they are not inclined to surrender, or even have opportunity to do so.

But psyops folks like to quote the pot of gold at the end of the rainbow – cumulative effect. 'it has not happened yet, but indicators are that it will soon...'

In Vietnam a great amount of effort went into creating broadcasts and leaflets to be scattered over places where the Vietcong/NVA were known to be or thought to be. The usual US analytical effort into quantifying effectiveness sometimes had surprising results.

Hundreds of thousands of leaflets with the Ace of Spades on them and a message to surrender or face a terrible death were printed and scattered. Prisoners and *hoi chanh* displayed a lack of appreciation of the powerful message on these leaflets and questioning found that the Ace of Spades had no special significance to Vietnamese.

Investigation revealed the entire program was the result of a US psyops person who watched a group of locals playing cards and the lively reaction of them when the Ace was played. It had an effect in that particular game, but not elsewhere.

Other leaflets were unknown to VC/NVA and *hoi chanh*. Investigation of this absence of knowledge about some leaflets revealed that they were printed at sea level in the moist conditions of Guam, then loaded into B-52s for dropping on targets. What no one considered was that the bales of leaflets froze into a solid block at the high altitudes flown by the B-52s, and when released, the leaflets were in the form of a giant ice block that hurtled down into the jungle.

Close combat

On one operation a headquarters group moved into a location while the rifle companies spread out to search assigned areas. A trail went past the position, so as a normal precaution, some weapons were placed a short distance along it. The M60 was in possession of a batman, who casually broke the ammunition belt so he had about ten rounds. Another batman had a 9mm Owen gun and the third man had his 7.62mm rifle, with a round in the breech.

All was quiet. Then, down the trail, some local people, hatless, with big packs appeared, walking fast, obviously on the way to market with something for sale. But as the locals got very close to the three Diggers, it became obvious that they were not farmers but Vietcong.

The machinegunner tried to fire but had a stoppage. The Owen gunner was so surprised he fired all 28 rounds and missed. The only man who did anything useful was the rifleman, who stepped forward, placed the muzzle of the rifle against the chest of the leading enemy, pulled the trigger and was dismayed to hear a 'click'. He had inadvertently picked up someone else's rifle.

The enemy scattered and were gone, and with them a chance for the headquarters to have a war story.

These people are
starving!
At Bien Hoa, the Intelligence Officer of 1RAR was driving around the various units in the city and came upon a US truck, with a big sergeant in the back throwing cans of food to an eager crowd of Vietnamese. The Australian stopped, approached the truck, identified himself and asked what the sergeant was doing. The American adopted an attitude of outraged righteousness and replied that,
'These people are starving! I am giving them food!'

The Australian asked if the sergeant knew what starving people looked like, and got the hesitant reply that he did not. The Aussie told the sergeant to look at the people, who were happy, smiling, chubby with fat cheeks and sparkling eyes, full of energy. Starving people are thin and listless with dull eyes.

The Aussie then pointed out the nearby lush rice fields, the water buffalo, and the orange orchards not far away, plus the street stalls selling a variety of food. The sergeant had driven past all this without 'seeing' any of it, and gave way to a desire to 'do good.'

The Aussie then completed the destruction of the sergeant's day by pointing out that food in tins was valued by the Vietcong, and whatever the sergeant had thrown to the crowd, unless eaten at once, would end up assisting the enemy, who would confiscate it, and who desired nothing more than to kill Americans.

Gourmets in the war zone

In the Australian logistics group base at Vung Tau someone formed a Gourmet's Club, which would meet in one of the many local restaurants, and an item on the menu would be the subject of a talk by one of the members.

An Aussie walking past a well-known beach-front restaurant saw a Military Policeman at the bar, and stopped for a chat. The MP was on duty, in civilian clothes, 9mm pistol in his waistband, as security for the Gourmet Club meeting, whose members could be seen at table in the dining area.

The MP was quietly enjoying his duty, as the special item on the menu that night was Napoleon cognac, and he had watched the necessary number of bottles handed to the restaurant manager, seen the first rounds poured and served, then been replaced by a lesser brand while the real Napoleon disappeared out the back. The gourmets never realised the deception.

Man's best friend

On Operation 'Silver City', C Company 1RAR was on the north bank of the Song Be (river) with a dismounted US cavalry unit employed as infantry on its left. The Vietcong had found they could creep towards the US position with a large locally made claymore mine, point it towards the noise from the cavalry units, retire and connect the electrical wires to send a blast of shrapnel into the US position.

C Company followed Australian procedures and patrolled, and also had standing patrols some distance to its front. One of these was comprised of four privates, each armed with the 7.62mm SLR. They saw a group of Vietcong approaching, waited, opened fire and were stunned by the resultant enormous explosion.

C Company sent a platoon to investigate. The Vietcong had been carrying one of their claymores and it had been detonated by a 7.62mm round. The explosion striped an area 35 paces across of foliage; the tree trunks were running with blood; human remains were scattered in the tree tops; a flattened area at the centre of blood trails showed where the survivors had spread a plastic sheet and carried to it pieces of bodies. One more wounded Vietcong was killed when he tried to open fire on the platoon.

Two days later a South Vietnamese tracker dog team arrived, to follow the trail of the survivors. The dog had been trained by the US Army, given to the South Vietnamese, and worked with US, South Korean and South Vietnamese units.

The dog seemed happy with his new friends and a platoon set off, dog and handler in front, a rifle section, then the platoon sergeant and two more sections.

The dog trotted along, apparently enjoying a walk in the bush, went right through the middle of the explosion site, that now smelled badly, and out the other side, happy as could be, with no sign that the site was in any way of interest.

About 50 yards (metres) on, the dog suddenly stopped and its attitude changed, it became alert, ears forward, then spun around and 'pointed' to indicate 'enemy' – straight at the platoon sergeant! The patrol continued with dog and handler at the rear.

Rations
The Aussies noticed that the dog handlers fed the dogs from the issue C Rations, but retained all the meat items for themselves and gave the dogs the biscuits, pound cake, pecan cake and similar.

It was also noticed that if any Vietnamese was in a position to exploit any other, he did so. Two Vietnamese were attached to 1RAR for an operation; one could speak and read some English. After some days, the other Vietnamese complained to one of the linguists about the rations and said he wanted to eat something other than biscuits. Investigation showed the other one had carefully removed from the ration boxes all the meat items and given his fellow soldier the rest.

We will fight with short hair

1RAR deployed out of Phuoc Tuy to assist in repelling the VC/NVA attacks in the Tet Offensive. After some weeks in the field, without access to a barber, long hair began to be noticeable. But the old network of senior NCOs and warrant officers came into effect.

The Company Sergeant Major (CSM) of D Company 1RAR telephoned a friend in Saigon and asked for a barber set to be bought at the big PX in Cholon and sent to the battalion in the field. This was done, and at the battles around Fire Support Base 'Coral' in May and June 1968, D/1RAR had regulation short hair.

Vietcong currency:
'Central Committee
of the National Liberation
Front South Vietnam'
50 xu
(half a Piastre or Dong)

White smoke

During a village clearance operation, the people were being sent back out of possible danger while the searching continued. A helicopter flew in and called for smoke to indicate the relevant landing site. Someone said,
'I've got one'

There was a click and hiss as the grenade activated, and a second voice said,
'I did not know we had white smoke.'

It was tear gas, and soon everyone was coughing, with watery stinging eyes and cursing the ancestry of the eager person who threw the grenade. Then there appeared a bunch of women and children coming back, led by a matriarch striding along at their head.

Despite the warning cries and waving gestures to stop, she led her crowd into the white mist, and soon the children were wailing and crying, the other women were distraught, and at their head the old woman strode along, loudly denigrating stupid men, their wars, their interference with daily life, their general uselessness and the weeping mass went past the partly amused and partly chastened Aussies.

It's not official issue,
but it is very useful
The Australian cavalry unit at Nui Dat had a very large 'walk-in' refrigerator, the envy of other units around, as the Australian government did not have such items available for issue in South Vietnam.

The cavalry acquired it by an example of quick thinking. One of the trucks was in Saigon, down by the docks at the river, where all ships unloaded. The driver noticed a long line of military trucks on the wharf alongside a freighter, from which the large refrigerators were being unloaded onto the trucks. The Aussie simply joined the queue, received a fridge, signed illegibly, and drove away to Nui Dat and the appreciation of all at the unit.

Well, yes, it's a war
zone, but there are
other important things
At one time the RSM of a small Aussie specialist unit at Vung Tau was a typical product of a peacetime career with promotion due to total observance of rules and regulations, and so elevation beyond his level of competence. His interest in newly arriving senior NCOs and warrant officers was whether they played darts. Lack of interest was not welcomed.

Like many of his ilk, he had childish ways of expressing displeasure, and one was to order the person to move into a room for the unpopular, so that at one time there were five sergeants and warrant officers in a room intended for two. This was borne with equanimity, as the RSM was like everyone else and would return to Australia in due course.

The Orbat Bigot
At headquarters 1ATF a corporal on the Intelligence staff was assigned to maintain the files on enemy Order of Battle, 'Orbat' in the vernacular. Over time, the 1ATF tactics and procedures resulted in a good collection of detail about the VC/NVA units in the region.

Captured documents, interrogations and de-briefs of surrendered enemy (*'hoi chanh'*) provided personal detail of enemy, sometimes to the extent of including the type of weapon on issue and its serial number.

Human nature being what it is, in time a particular corporal became so convinced his files were correct in detail that he became known as 'the orbat bigot'. When the Vietcong surrendered to the Australian laundry vehicle, as he was in a support organisation for some years, he had not been mentioned in any captured document nor by any *hoi chanh*.

There then arose the farcical situation of a surrendered enemy having to prove his existence to the corporal orbat bigot.

However, the corporal was diligent, and over time came to suspect, then to believe, that one of the two Vietcong Local Force battalions in the 1ATF area had been disbanded, due to casualties and lack of recruits, with NVA infiltrators placed into all units to keep some force in existence. The two battalions were D440 and D445. D440 had been an unhappy outfit due to clashes between the Southerners and Northerners, the age-old source of enmity between the regions.

Eventually it was found to be so – D440 had ceased to exist. However, the corporal was neither thanked nor officially recognised for his work, as this would have meant recognising also the failure of the officers concerned in identifying this significant development.

Dustoff

'Dustoff' was the famous radio call sign for medical evacuation helicopters in the Vietnam War.

Someone with too much idle time came up with the meaning of this to be 'Dedicated Untiring Support for Our Fighting Forces'. This is untrue.

When US aviation first began operations in South Vietnam, aircraft were designated on radio by the tail number, such as 'Army 4567'. But as the involvement increased, a more authoritative system was instituted, with call signs allocated to various units.

The helicopter medical evacuation unit happened to be allocated 'Dustoff' as it was on the list of available call signs, and eventually all such flights came to be 'Dustoff'.

*This is an Intelligence
briefing*

On 1RAR's second tour of duty in SVN, the Intelligence sergeant was a well-known battalion character. Periodically, officers from Reserve units – at the time, Citizen Military Force (CMF) – would arrive for a stay to observe how operations were conducted, lessons learned and similar, for use back in Australia with their own units. It also gave them a sense of being included in the Regular Army's activities.

The Intelligence sergeant would be required to give these groups a briefing on the situation in the Australian area, and sometimes added 'extras' to add to the interest of the visit. The visitors accepted what they were told, and returned to Australia none the wiser.

On one occasion the sergeant pointed to the map and listed the US, Free World, South Vietnamese and Australian units, the air assets available, and the off-shore naval forces which could contribute gunfire if requested. He tapped a point on the map just off-shore and casually added that the battleship USS *Missouri* was there with its huge guns.

One of the visitors piped up and said he thought the battleship was well to the north, near the DMZ.

The sergeant looked at him, asked where that information came from, and was told the magazine '*Newsweek*'.

The sergeant emanated the invincible authority of a man in possession of the facts, and turned away, back to the map, with the crushing remark,
'**This** is an Intelligence briefing!'

The three types
There seemed to be three types of people in the Australian Army of the time. There were those who had been in for years, during several wars, but somehow had not had any war service. Their medal ribbons were for long service, the British Long Service and Good Conduct (LS&GCM) or Meritorious Service Medal (MSM). Ability to avoid going to a war resulted in being described as having 'gang-plank fever' – an illness that prevented climbing a gang-plank into a troopship. They were able to wear the uniform, receive military pay and avoid war service, serve until retirement age, and leave. These are rarely seen in veterans' associations or at reunions.

There were those who enlisted, went on war service if sent, never volunteered, wore their war service medals and avoided any further time in a combat area, often by being downgraded medically. Some of these magically improved in health after the involvement in South Vietnam ended.

An example of the other sort of injured soldier was one of the original linguists with 1RAR 1965-66, who had been burned on one arm and on part of his torso in a traffic accident in 1964. In May 1965 he was posted to 1RAR and departed for South Vietnam in the first Qantas flight. In about April 1966 the battalion doctor was informed that this sergeant was unfit for war service or service in the tropics.

The third type was of the people who volunteered for tours of duty in the war zone, whatever it was. People on their second, third or subsequent tours of duty in South Vietnam met each other frequently, and this group comprised a small club, with no signs, badges or office bearers, but who knew each other by reputation.

A few, with no family ties, stayed in Vietnam for years. One linguist was in Vung tau for five years, and a warrant officer with the advisory training team also served there for five years. Some regulars did two 12-month tours of duty, many did three. Of course, marriages suffered.

The pop music
The popular music of the time remains with the veterans and families, and stirs memories of people, places and events. In some units a list of top pops or well-known songs from film, stage or operetta, and units to which these supposedly referred, generated some smiles. Performers of the times included The Beatles, Creedence Clearwater Revival, the Beach Boys, Tom Jones, Frank Sinatra, Dean Martin, Diana Ross and the Supremes, the Animals, the Rolling Stones, Jefferson Airplane and many others.

I hope her aim
was good
An Aussie had oral sex performed on him and after the girl brought him to climax she spat over the side of the bed. His first thought was, 'My shoes are down there!'

Be first with the news
These two incidents actually happened in 1970 at the headquarters of the

First Australian Task Force (1ATF).

The Maori reputation
The Australians had individuals and contingents of high-performing New Zealanders incorporated into the force, including officers on the headquarters staff.

A New Zealand rifle company was tracking and engaging a Vietcong unit, with small actions being fought over successive days. One morning there was an action and the results reported by wireless with the number of enemy killed, and a small number wounded.

At about mid-day, an Australian officer walked into the command post just as the New Zealanders out in the bush reported that the wounded enemy had died. A NZ officer in the CP looked at the clock, and said, knowingly, that it was lunch-time, so the Maoris were preparing to eat the enemy.

The Australian officer stopped, shocked at this news, and ran to the office of the Brigadier commanding 1ATF, with, 'Sir! War atrocities! The Maoris are eating enemy!'

The elephant farm
The US forces in the region were constantly looking for evidence of enemy use of elephants as load-carriers along the jungle tracks. The Vietnamese did not use elephants as did their neighbours, but the search was constant.

The Australians did not pay much attention to this requirement, but one day a US helicopter delivered an elephant skull to the Nui Dat helicopter landing zone of the Australian commander. This promptly was taken, put on a cement base and white-washed, in best military style. The Australian psychological operations unit created a cartoon of a big elephant cocking its leg over the US base camp and scattered these over that camp.

The fun continued, with cartoons showing elephants prepared to launch spears from the trunk, and nubile Vietnamese girls washing in a river with surprised looks, but a smirking elephant behind them, trunk in the water.

The search for elephants resulted in a spurious report of a translation of a captured Vietcong document that indicated honours and awards for service to an elephant-raising unit supposedly located on a very small island, four km by two km, close to the mainland near the swamps at the mouth of the Saigon River. The document included many clues – the unit was the *B747*, and the Boeing airliner, the' Jumbo jet' was newly in service; one unit commander was *Nguyen Jum Bo*; another was *Trun Kan Toe*.

The same officer who rushed to report the Maori cannibalism saw this 'report' and again rushed to inform the commander that elephants were being bred on the tiny island. One glance at the map and at the 'report' generated a loud, 'GET OUT!'

Keep your cool,
live longer
This could be the
equivalent of an
urban myth.

Reportedly the Australian sense of humour extended to SAS ambushes. In the killing zone along a track or trail a stick would be left upright in plain view with a note slipped into a small cut in the end. This note would say, in Vietnamese, *'Greetings. You are in an Australian ambush'* and fire would be opened when the victims halted while the leading enemy opened and read the note.

The story goes that one such leading Vietcong saw the note, read it, and with no change in facial expression, turned and passed it to the man behind him, then leaped forward at top speed and fled the ambush, the sole survivor.

The meat pies – the
whole task force upset

A traditional Aussie part of enjoying the football or cricket is a meat pie, with sauce. The Victorian football League (VFL) arranged for a supply of frozen pies to be flown to 1ATF, enough for everyone there. Unfortunately, these were mistakenly unloaded en route, thawed, and were ruined. There was disappointment all around.

A Warrant Officer Class 2, with a devious sense of humour, drafted a notice to all units at Nui Dat that a second consignment of pies was on the way, with the detail of the date and location of serving. The pies would be available at the office of the 1ATF Amenities Officer, be served hot, and all units were to inform him of the number of pies needed.

As in any bureaucracy, something on paper has a life of its own and is given some value. So it was with this item.

The hapless amenities officer soon was receiving calls from every unit at Nui Dat, and his protests were ignored. Human nature being what it is, suspicion developed that the pies were to be 'stolen' from the deserving soldiery and consumed by the rear echelon and headquarters people not at Nui Dat. The Amenities Officer began to receive threats.

On the nominated day, the area around the amenities Office was clogged with troops from all the resident units – engineers in big earth-moving vehicles and trucks, jeeps, Landrovers – all demanding hot pies. A platoon of 2RAR, faces blackened, about to go on patrol, walked down to get their hot pies. The garrison military police had to be brought in to disperse the crowd.

The inevitable backlash began. Who had done this? There seemed to be no answer, until the chief clerk at 1ATF recalled one day seeing a corporal from the Divisional Intelligence Unit detachment putting something in the rack of mail boxes for the 1ATF units – 'and they don't do that.'

So the officer commanding the detachment had an 'interview' with the Brigadier and a firm order to confine unit jokes to the unit and to not upset the whole task force. The detachment had been responsible for the 'elephant farm' debacle.

But for weeks at conferences people would produce the piece of paper and ask about the pies…..

What am I *doing* here…?

The 1ATF area of operations did not include the port city of Vung Tau, which was out of bounds unless on leave or official duty. The commander of the 1ATF Intelligence detachment, on his second tour of duty, was passing through Vung Tau when he noticed a Land-Rover parked outside a bar. The vehicle had the distinctive fitting of loudspeakers on the cabin roof, so identifying it as from the 1ATF psyops unit.

In the bar, in uniform, was a senior NCO from the unit. The officer asked what the NCO was doing and was told that he was
'Collecting sociological Intelligence.'

It was exactly the wrong pathetic answer. The NCO was told to get out of the city and back across the bridge into the 1ATF area. But we have not heard the last of this fellow.

Beware of warrant officers trying to fool young officers

The warrant officer at the Air Intelligence cell at 1ATF had a visitor one day. A lieutenant from a battalion requested an air photo coverage of the battalion area of operations, to the scale of 1:5,000, to fit on a clip-board.

Now, this sounds like a typical joke about dense subalterns, but it is true. The warrant officer explained that the air photos could be produced and supplied, but a scale of one to five thousand meant that one inch or centimetre of the clip-board would represent five thousand, so it was impossible.

The subaltern was well aware of the ways in which senior NCOs and warrant officers conspired to make young officers look foolish, and insisted that his requirement be met. It was, after all, for the benefit of a combat battalion and the job of the staff was to support the infantry.

No matter how the warrant officer tried to explain the ratio between scales and clip-board size, the lieutenant insisted.

The farce deepened. The warrant officer asked if the lieutenant would believe a senior officer, and he agreed to hear from the Major in the next office. This was the same officer who believed the Maoris were eating prisoners and elephants were bred on the off-shore island. You know what happened next!

The major agreed with the lieutenant and told the warrant officer to do as requested.... In desperation, the warrant officer suggested another telephone call: to the lieutenant colonel commanding a US aerial reconnaissance support battalion, who finally convinced both the major and lieutenant of the stupidity of the original request.

Cultural differences

- 5

Over the years of US involvement enthusiasm for involvement in the war decreased markedly. The repeated battles for a piece of ground that was taken and abandoned then had to be taken again resulted in loss of morale. No matter how many enemy were 'counted' killed, more seemed to be out there in the jungle.

Decisions by US Secretary of Defense Robert MacNamara and his 'whiz kids' in Washington DC were to the detriment of the US forces. 'Cost effectiveness' resulted in mass production of cheaper fuses for munitions, which resulted in bombs and shells that failed to detonate, and so provided the Vietcong with large amounts of high explosive when the bombs and shells were painstakingly hacksawed open – as shown in Vietcong films.

The decision to replace the US forces in South Vietnam on an individual basis, the 'trickle feed' program, rather than rotate units as a whole, was a disaster. Every man in a US unit, from commander down to the lowest ranked trooper, arrived as an individual who had to establish a working relationship with those around him.

The tour of duty was one year, or '365 days and a wakey' in terminology of the time. So at some time, the commander was the newest man in the unit.

The Australians and New Zealanders rotated units, in which everyone knew the others, had trained together, travelled overseas together and settled into the base together. There was a sense of belonging to an organisation that worked with a sense of purpose. Historical studies showed that combat soldiers performed well for their comrades, their fellows in arms, but did not do so well at all in company of strangers.

The US system had officers do half a tour in a field position and then half a tour on the staff, and this dislocated unit cohesiveness.

In later years, US officers and senior NCOs were murdered by reluctant soldiers – 'fragged' by a grenade – and it was known that this was done because the average US soldier did not want to go out on aggressive operations. Many would fight in self- defence, but not go looking for trouble.

Racial problems were added to the mix, along with 'peace' signs and love beads; drugs were readily available. The US force in South Vietnam in 1970-71 was not the same eager force of 1965-66.

The Australian-New Zealand task force continued to operate, and to patrol and ambush aggressively and destroyed the enemy in Phuoc Tuy Province, which had to be replaced by 33 NVA Regiment, and that unit remained in occupation after 1975.

In 1970-71 US officers visited 1ATF to see what the differences were, and why this small contingent, with conscripts and Regulars, continued to seek out the enemy without morale problems, without 'fragging', and what seemed the same level of enthusiasm as in 1965.

The Hoa Long dance
A long-running joke at the 1ATF base was 'the Hoa Long Dance'. Soon after the Australians settled into the Nui Dat base, in the nearby town of Hoa Long a sign appeared outside the local rice mill: *'Dance Saturday night. 50-50'.* This was shown to new arrivals as the vehicle went past, and the new guys informed there really was a country dance, with a band and local girls, just like back home in Australia. The dance was highly rated, very enjoyable, and some local girls were said to be very good-looking.

Anyone wishing to attend was to notify the unit headquarters and appear on a small parade, suitably dressed, then move to the central gathering to board trucks for the dance.

The central gathering was at the 1ATF Military Police unit, where the dress and neatness of all those going to the dance would be inspected by a military police officer or warrant officer. Officers would not have to undergo inspection, but were taken aside, into the military police unit bar (yes, junior officers fell for this like many others!)

Inevitably, the inspection would find fault with everyone on parade and each man would be sent back to his unit, there to be the subject of jokes and unfeeling remarks from the veterans. However, everyone became part of the joke and the secret never leaked to new arrivals.

It is a fact that one gullible corporal tried three times to go to the dance, and was refused each time. He then wrote to the task force commander about the injustice of the arrangement by which the officers were allowed to go to the dance every Saturday night – having seen them taken away at the parade - but the junior ranks were kept back.

The Dat Do Dogs
A similar joke was the supposed greyhound races at the local town of Dat Do, but was never as successful as the Hoa Long dance.

The Baria RSL
Another trap for the innocent was the advice that a sub-branch of the Australian Returned Service League (RSL), for veterans, was in the province capital of Baria. Once people had enough time in service in the war zone to qualify for membership of the RSL, an application could be sent via unit headquarters to join.

The corporal who tried to go to the dance also applied to join the RSL at Baria, but so did others did so over the years.

Start digging
Some of the CMF or Reserve officers who came on a visit to the Australian force had become accustomed to enjoying the privileges of rank in their unit at home. One lieutenant-colonel of artillery arrived at a fire support base in the afternoon, was welcomed and given a briefing. Things were proceeding well and everyone around was busy, attending to their duties, when Vietcong mortaring began.

The visitor asked for a soldier to dig his pit, and was brought to reality when informed that everyone, regardless of rank, dug their own in the field, and no Digger was going to be allocated to him for anything. There was some quiet amusement among the Regulars at the sight of a CMF lieutenant-colonel applying himself to getting below ground level.

Logistics
On Operation 'Silver City' in March 1966, large caches of bagged rice were found and it was decided to use big twin-rotor Chinook helicopters to bring Mechanical Mules, small four-wheeled load carriers to take the rice to a clearing so it could be flown back to be handed to the government.

At the 1RAR headquarters a newly arrived officer noticed the stream of Chinooks passing and asked what they were doing. He was told they were flying in 'Mules' to evacuate the rice, pondered this for a moment, and, a graduate of the Royal Military College Duntroon, considered the logistics aspect of mules in South Vietnam, and asked,

'But where are they going to get fodder for them?'

The water buffalo
Anyone on patrol near farming areas in South Vietnam soon realised that water buffalo, used for ploughing and pulling carts, became disturbed by the nearness of foreign troops, because of odour. It was a source of amusement that these big animals were cared for by local children, who were not awed by the size of their charges. But if Australian or US troops appeared, often the animals would become disturbed, stamp, toss their horns, and show some signs of aggressiveness.

When 1RAR was clearing the towns in the La Nga valley on Operation 'New Life', a buffalo broke loose and charged, scattering Aussies left and right. One Digger ran ahead of the beast then stepped aside, but as it went past, hit it on the head with the butt of his M79 grenade launcher.

The weapon fired and a 40mm high explosive grenade sailed up and away and by the fortunes of war landed in the battalion headquarters, which then expected a successive rain of missiles. There was some surprise when no more arrived.

This was a platoon secret for 25 years, until a history of the tour of duty was written.

Dehydrated Water pills
The Australian anti-malaria medication was a daily Paludrine pill, which was swallowed with a sip of water, as it had a very unpleasant taste. The same gullible soldier who tried three times to go to the Hoa Long dance and to join the Baria RSL also was seen thoughtfully chewing a paludrine tablet after being told they were 'dehydrated water' pills.

The Big Voice from
On High
B-52 strikes, called 'Arc Light', were notified ahead of arrival to various headquarters. The effect of these bombing runs was spectacular, as the aircraft were too high to be heard and the first sign of their presence was a string of explosions from large bombs.

One Australian officer who knew of B-52 attacks made a practice of having a light observation plane available, and would circle off to a side, wait for the string of explosions, and then dive along the bomb-path, announcing through a loud-hailer,

'BUDDHA IS ANGRY!'

The Big Voice from
On High - 2

One action used in counter-revolutionary warfare was the 'cordon and search'. A village or small town, or a suburb would be cordoned off and each building searched thoroughly, while the entire population was moved to a central area and their identification checked. This involved lot of planning and participation by many different types of units, from combat elements to medical, psychological warfare, Intelligence, transport, and government representatives.

After the cordon had silently surrounded the village, and before the locals awoke and began to disperse into the fields, at the right moment a message in Vietnamese would be broadcast from a helicopter or fixed wing aircraft. This would inform the people an operation had begun, they were not to go into the fields or forest, but to take all their identification documents and move to the village square or market place.

A cordon and search was planned for the village of Ngai Giao, north of the Nui Dat base of 1ATF in July 1968.

The Australian Army helicopter duly took off in the early morning darkness, flew to the correct location and began to transmit the message, from a tape supplied by 1ATF. As the light grew, the pilot could see the local people obediently leaving home and going to the market place. He thought the cordon and search troops were very well camouflaged, because he could not see any of them. He could not see any government or Australian people in and around the market place either.

At the appointed time, he returned to base and reported what had happened. A phone call to 1ATF created furore. The cordon and search was not until the next day. A tape had to be made quickly and flown over the village, to allow the people to get on with their day.

An attempt was made to pin the blame on the Army pilot, but a check showed the order from 1ATF had the incorrect date and time. Reportedly a staff officer was sent home in disgrace.

We'll have it waiting
for you back home

The Aussies were impressed by the size and scope of the US military presence, and also by the presence of salesmen for US products, mainly automobiles, in the war zone.

The Aussies were amazed to find that US servicemen could order a particular model of car, with nominated colour, tyres, special fittings, whatever was desired, to be available at a specified address for their collection on return from Vietnam.

Customer identification

Another surprising aspect of commercial activity was the almost perfect ability of the Indian shop-keepers, usually tailors or jewellers, to see an approaching US, Aussie or New Zealander in civilian clothes and be able to address each correctly by nationality.

Everyone had short military haircuts, wore the same locally bought casual civilian clothes on leave, but had some minor but significant characteristics the astute businessman could identify.

A general and a dog

After a successful action in 1968, 1RAR was warned that General Creighton Abrams, MACV commander, would visit the unit. There was the usual order to improve neatness in the position, and for everyone to be shaved, 'bright, clean and lightly oiled' as the saying went, ready for the important visitor.

During his tour of the position, Abrams came to the location of the Tracker Dog platoon. The dogs and handlers were lined up along the track. As soon as Abrams saw the dogs, he stopped, and asked if they were attack dogs.

The battalion commander and platoon commander assured him that these were dogs that only tracked a scent, and were harmless – they would not attack anyone.

Abrams moved closer and as soon as he was within reach, the closest dog leaped forward and sank his teeth into Abrams' calf.

In the middle of the 1RAR position the senior US general was hopping around with an Australian dog attached to his leg, a horrified hander trying to order the dog to let go, various appalled staff officers trying to help, the Australian generals looking at the battalion commander, who was glaring at the second lieutenant platoon commander, who wondered about his future career in the military.

Abrams limped away. The Vietcong missed out on a great story.

My orders include
you, colonel
During the fighting in Saigon in the Tet Offensive, for a time infiltrating Vietcong could be expected anywhere. The Australian commander prudently ordered that no one was to leave the headquarters without wearing a helmet, a flak jacket, equipment and a weapon, in case of involvement in a street action.

A self-important colonel, not wearing any of the above items, was called back from the gate to the general's office and forcefully reminded of his requirement to set an example to the junior ranks, and obey orders.

Armies being the same everywhere, there were quiet smiles among the troops at the sight of the colonel in helmet, flak jacket and carrying a weapon.

What are you made of?
During a night action at Fire Support Base 'Coral', 1968, an Engineer officer running crouched at top speed through a mortar bombardment collided with a Sapper running the opposite way. The officer started to check himself for damage in the collision and the Sapper casually said,
'Oh, blokes like you don't bleed.'

Anticipating a compliment on his professional toughness, the officer asked what was meant, and the sapper continued,
'Officers are full of shit.'

It's all in the mind
During Operation 'Crimp', at night the Vietcong would attempt to mortar the US-Australian positions, with great lack of success. Two Aussies later smiled at their attitude to enemy and friendly fire at the time.

When on sentry on the machine gun, they would sit up on the back of the fighting pit, for a better view to their front, and ignore the scattered mortar explosions.

The artillery well to the rear would fire flares on request, and these would arrive overhead, with a distinctive sound as the flare separated from the container and continued to the point when it ignited the flare, and the container whistled its way down to impact somewhere in or near the night position. Whenever this happened, the pair would slip down into the pit until the container thumped down.

But when their sentry time was over, they would go back to sleep without worrying about either enemy mortars or friendly flare containers.

If you've finished your
coffee, your helicopter
is waiting

A US general achieved success in his first command in South Vietnam by allocating to each of his battalion commanders a quota of enemy to be killed. Every dead person that resulted from this order was a Vietcong and the performance of the formation was noted. The general went back to the USA, was promoted, and in due course returned to higher command in Vietnam.

He applied the same quotas to his subordinate units, which this time included 1ATF.

When the Australians and New Zealanders did not achieve their quotas, the general flew to Nui Dat, resplendent in his star-covered uniform, determined to bring the Aussies up to his standard of performance. 1ATF was under US operational control, but that was all. Administration, discipline, every army matter, remained under Australian control. How and what 1ATF did in its allocated area was an Australian matter.

The general delivered his talk, demanded more enemy killed each week, the figure to be reported to his headquarters, and reportedly was infuriated by the attitude of the Australian commander, who quietly said that 1ATF did not operate like that, security had been improved greatly in the region, and the general's helicopter was waiting for him.

Who are you, really?

Depending on the attitude of the 1ATF commander, the Intelligence detachment conducted raids, known as *'Acorn operations'*, into the local towns and villages to capture Vietcong, who then were interrogated and handed over to the local government.

On one such raid, at night, one senior NCO found himself alone, with the prisoner, in Hoa Long town, and decided to notify others on the raid of his movements because of the danger of friendly fire. But then he found that he could not remember the radio call sign, thought about it, remembered, and announced that he was making his way with the prisoner to the assigned gathering place.

Rather than the reply being in the voice of one of the Intelligence unit, a stranger answered and asked for verification. More transmissions followed, the raiders gathered and returned to 1ATF with the prisoner.

Higher ranks and signals staff were waiting, because the call sign used was the personal one for the 1ATF commander, and there was consternation at the headquarters when apparently the commander was alone in the middle of Hoa Long with a prisoner.....

Where angels
fear to tread

The advisors in Hoa Long also were infuriated when informed of this debacle, because they had not been informed of the raid, launched on very short notice, and the raiders had passed through several places where South Vietnamese defences were supposed to be in ambush. No one was there. The Hoa Long defenders had decided to not go out and lose sleep that night … as on many other occasions.

Strangers in the night

Another Acorn operation was made on the basis of information from a surrendered Vietcong, a 'rallier', who offered to lead a raid to a house where two other Vietcong were hiding, but this had to be done quickly as the two would not be there for long. A raid comprising Australians, South Vietnamese and their US advisers was rapidly organised and the force set off at speed for the town. The internal roads shrank to paths and the vehicles had to be left while the raid strung out behind the rallier.

There was some surprise for those in the rear when those at the front appeared on their right, to be told that the rallier had only ever been to the house at night, and now was navigating by remembering the shape of the trees silhouetted against the night sky.

Patience was required, and the rallier went off, staring skywards, along paths between homes. Then he stopped and pointed to a house. The raid surrounded it and the South Vietnamese rushed inside, grabbed the family and dragged them out to the porch, with lots of shouting and threats and fervent denials by the family.

The rallier was standing quietly by the Australian commander of the detachment, then tugged his sleeve and started trying to tell him something – he had made a mistake and it was the house next door!

The 'innocents' were abandoned and the shouting South Vietnamese – very much in Keystone Kops mode – repeated the performance, and, sure enough, two Vietcong were found in a hiding place under the bathroom floor.

There is a quota for
these things, you know
The Intelligence detachment at 1ATF had been successful in a series of raids against the important Vietcong Infrastructure (VCI), the basis on which the organisation operated.

The detachment commander thought some recognition was due so went to 1ATF headquarters to discuss award of some medals for his men. He was told to forget it, as he had only twenty-six people in the detachment, and the quota for awards was one Mention in Dispatches (MID) per 200 men per six months. The detachment would need to be there for eight years before even a recommendation for a MID could be made, and that might be quashed at higher headquarters.

It is a fact that a post-war survey of Australian awards for service in South Vietnam by a military historical society found that an award was more likely to be made for activity some distance from the enemy than closer to him. The survey showed the RAN awarded the most, then the RAAF, with Army last, and among them the headquarters in Saigon received more than the combat units.

Well, I just wanted to have a shot or two...
A platoon of 2RAR was resting in the mid-day heat during a patrol and minding its own business. Suddenly shots were heard and the bullets were going into the bush around and above the platoon.

Careful peering around found an Australian Army Land-Rover parked in the distance and from it shots were fired into the surrounds. It was easy to identify the unit, because on the cabin roof were the distinctive loud-speakers of the psyops unit, and the number plate was visible.

Once again, the senior NCO who had taken time off on duty to go to Vung Tau and meet bar girls as a source of 'sociological Intelligence' was present as the shooter.

Denials were useless as the platoon definitely reported the vehicle identification.

We want to be their
friends and mentors
The trend to lessen the military aspect of warfare and increase the 'friendly persuasion' aspect – in direct defiance of the lessons of history – had a senior officer quoted as saying words to the effect of the Army should train people to be good at agricultural matters so they could be deployed to assist the locals raise better crops and animals.

Somehow this did not result in a major change in Defence.

Tet 1968
The war in South Vietnam had an unusual feature – truces for significant national events, when fighting would cease, enemies would make family visits, normal curfew would be relaxed, and a semblance of peace-time living would be enjoyed. The main one of these truces as over the Lunar New Year, '*Tet*'. The overall situation for the Communist regime in Hanoi was bad, and it was decided to launch a major offensive over Tet 1968, *Tet Mau Than*, the Year of the Monkey.

There were parties and celebrations everywhere, and the various embassies had their own 'Tet parties'. At the end of one of these, a number of people from the Australian embassy were being driven home, and one of them commented on the large crowds in the streets, with the remark that there could be Vietcong among them going about their business.

A member of the military attaché staff was in the car, and explained about the truce, that it happened every year, and that there probably were Vietcong among the crowd but they would be on their way home to celebrate. Two hours later the Tet Offensive began, the turning point in the involvement by the USA and Free World Forces in the war in South Vietnam.

Tet 1968 – 2
The member of the military attaché staff was peacefully asleep soon after, when there was a loud noise nearby. His wife asked what it was, and he made what almost fit the category of 'famous last words': 'Thunder'. His wife pointed out that it was the dry season and there was not a storm for 500 miles in any direction.

Immediately there was another burst of 'thunder' nearby, and he was now fully awake, and very conscious of the fact that embassy staff were unarmed and there seemed to be gun battles to the left and to the right – the US Embassy and the Independence Palace. There was nothing to do but wait for dawn, in the company of the neighbouring Commonwealth Police Sergeant. There then began a very busy time for the office of the military attaché.

The US Embassy
Saigon
A great amount of drivel was written and broadcast by the media during the war in Vietnam, and especially so during Tet 68. The quite untrue breathless reports of Vietcong attackers having gained entry into the US Embassy were relayed without checking, originated by media wannabes who sneaked a quick peek towards the embassy and filed rubbish.

The Vietcong did gain access to the compound by blowing holes in the street wall (the 'thunder') but the USMC guard immediately made sure the big wooden front doors of the embassy building were shit and locked. From the rooftop, security staff and USMC guards shot down at the enemy in the garden. One determined Vietcong actually reached the portico steps but was killed as he got there. Other Vietcong hid under huge ornamental 'saucers' that were a garden feature and died there.

Untrue reports that Vietcong were inside the embassy shooting outwards could have been disproved at once by anyone who had actually seen the embassy itself and thought about these wild statements. The building itself was protected by an outer wall of 'breeze blocks', cement blocks that allowed some light to pass, but provided protection from projectiles and blast. From inside the building there was no field of fire at all because of the outer wall.

In Hanoi there was despair, because the offensive had been defeated everywhere, but this turned to joy when it became obvious that US media reporting presented the attacks as a major victory.

What if..?

History is littered with examples of how the fortunes of generals, admirals, wartime opponents, business empires and governments and nations sometimes hinged on a relatively small event. It can be said that the outcome of the Vietnam war turned on one of these matters.

On Operation 'Crimp' in January 1966 the 173rd Airborne Brigade, with 1RAR, in the Cu Chi location, captured the headquarters of the Vietcong Military Region that covered the Saigon area. A tremendous haul of important documents, plus weapons and items of equipment was found in a tunnel network over the next week.

One item found was a satchel with a big folder that contained the full name and personal detail of every member of the Vietcong in the region. The detail had name, code name, place and date of birth, occupation, place of work, of residence, date of joining, assessment, any punishments awarded, and other detail. This was taken at once to the commander of 1RAR, contents explained, and sent to Saigon.

There it disappeared. It is not unreasonable to state that if the information in the folder had been exploited by the South Vietnamese the entire Vietcong organisation around Saigon would have been destroyed, or at least disrupted badly, with all those listed either arrested or forced to flee and hide. The whole operational base of the Vietcong in and around Saigon would have been set back for years.

It is not unreasonable to state that if this was so, then the Tet Offensive would not have included very much, if any, activity around Saigon. The whole thrust of media reporting in Tet 1968 would have been different.

It was not until September 1966 that the US was able to have combined US-South Vietnamese organisations created for the use of captured personnel, documents and equipment.

The media

There were hundreds of accredited media people in South Vietnam, from amateurs with a letter of authorisation from a couple of local newspapers somewhere, to hardened professionals with contacts into the higher levels of command and government.

In the Tet Offensive, the Vietcong repeatedly broadcast notices that such and such an area or location was under the control of the 'liberation' forces and access was denied. Some media representatives did not think this applied to them, but events took a nasty turn that resulted in the deaths of a jeep-load of journalists.

With all the military action around Saigon, the temptation to shoot ammunition as well as camera film became too much for two men, one Australian ex-army and one US ex-navy. Word got around, and so quickly to the Vietcong, that the two were firing at VC/NVA forces. The ex-USN man was killed in the action around Tansonnhut airbase when he remained standing instead of taking cover to clear a stoppage in his rifle.

A jeep-load of Australian and British journalists were killed in Saigon, after ignoring a warning from forward US troops that the enemy was around the street corner, and drove on. One man returned, to relate how a Vietcong with pistol walked up to them after a burst of fire, and despite cries of *'bao chi'* (journalist), calmly repeated it while firing at point-blank range. The survivor realised his only chance to escape came when the pistol was empty, took it and ran back around the corner.

This group-killing infuriated many in the media community, and a contract for the death of the Australian was reportedly 'open'. He lived a desperate life, unable to leave South Vietnam as the local police had his pass-port and used pressure on him from illegal financial exchanges to try to acquire damaging information about troublesome journalists, never sleeping in the same place on consecutive nights, and carried three pistols. Eventually he flew to Cambodia when the US forces invaded there to attack the huge headquarters and supply complex of the VC/NVA, and back to Australia.

The exotic East
North-east of Bien Hoa on the bank of the Dong Nai there was an area infested with leeches. They were in such numbers that the leaves seemed to move as thousands of leeches reared up seeking the source of body heat that attracted them. They could be seen in their thousands moving towards their prey.

The usual remedy of holding a lighted cigarette to them to make them drop off was not practical in operational circumstances. A man would look down and see what looked like a bunch of grapes hanging from a place on his trouser leg. A squirt of mosquito repellent worked well. Then men were seen with lower trouser legs stiff with dried blood.

It was agreed that the Vietcong were welcome to the place, but some wondered why there were so many leeches in that place and what they fed on before the Aussies arrived.

Rules is rules
On Operation 'Junction City', US forces captured a large quantity of documents, equipment, and some Vietcong films that showed them 'in their natural state', planning attacks, logistics efforts, crossing rivers, holding political meetings, and even some US Army prisoners from early years.

Copies of the films were made for each of the nations with an embassy in Saigon, and these were distributed by the liaison office. The military attaché office at the Australian Embassy (Austemba) collected the films, along with other material, and sent them off to Canberra, to the Directorate of Military Intelligence (DMI).

The following sequence of messages was sent:
DMI
What is the security
classification of the
captured films?

Austemba
None. The US has
made copies for
everyone here and
they are not classified.
DMI
These are captured
enemy material and
must be classified.
Austemba
All other embassies
have copies with no
classification.
DMI
Repeats request for
classification of captured
enemy material.
Austemba
Make them *'Restricted'*.
DMI
'Restricted' not high enough.
Austemba
Make them *'Confidential'*.

So the films were classified 'Confidential', and sent to the School of Military Intelligence, where they were used for training courses for the remainder of the time that Australia was involved in the Vietnam War, after which they sat in a container, unused.

In the mid-1980s an Australian film writer became interested in making a film about the Battle of Long Tan, and in his conversations with veterans was told of the existence of the captured films. These would be very useful for seeing how the Vietcong dressed, what weapons they carried, and how they 'looked'. The films were traced to SMI, and then began an exercise in bureaucracy.

The films were from a foreign source – USA – and were classified, so could not be released until they were declassified. The point that the classification was at the insistence of DMI in 1968 was ignored – the relevant paper-work showed the films came from a US source.

A hapless Australian officer from the embassy in Washington DC then was tasked to contact the relevant US authority and request declassification of the films. The obvious US response was that the USA never had classified the films, so had no authority to declassify them.

Stalemate. The films were at SMI and, in theory, never could be declassified.

The problem was resolved by an officer at SMI, a man promoted through the ranks, who used his authority delegated by Her Majesty Queen Elizabeth II, declared the films to be declassified, completed the necessary paper-work and sent the films to the Australian War Memorial, Canberra, for public use.

Of course, bureaucrats everywhere go to their graves smugly confident that they have always obeyed the rules, never exceeded their authority and never made a decision that was not supported by the official book. Every society has them.

A ruined day after
Vietnam
One of the two linguists with 1RAR 1965-66 was to return in 1967 and had to attend a series of briefings in Canberra on his coming duties. One briefing was in a building at Defence, where a corporal met him and conducted him through along corridors and through doors which could be opened only by tapping the secret numbers of a keypad, over which the officious corporal hunched to obscure the view of the visitor.

The linguist, a sergeant, was shown into the office of a colonel, who invited him to be seated, opened a file on the desk, fixed the visitor with a serious look, and said that he now officially informed him that Australia and its allies intercepted enemy radio communications.

The sergeant's response began ruination of the colonel's day. He said, 'Oh, I know that, sir.'

The colonel reared back. 'How do *you* know that?'

The sergeant explained that at Bien Hoa, 1RAR was accompanied on operations by US troops with radios who provided information on what they intercepted. The colonel was dismayed, and asked who else knew this, and the reply made him even more dismayed. The sergeant said that probably everyone in 1RAR knew, and so did the artillery and armour people who also went on operations.

The colonel sat back in his chair, quite obviously deeply concerned. The sergeant did not cheer up the colonel when he said that the US unit was in brigade headquarters with its own compound, at which a large sign advised its identity, and the unit jeeps carried on the spare wheel cover the identity of the person who had use of that jeep.

The colonel was deeply dismayed at this, and quite obviously was wondering how such a huge breach of security could be remedied. The sergeant signed the relevant forms to signify that he had been briefed on the matter, and left a very sad senior officer.

The colonel presumably was unaware that the very first US soldier killed in South Vietnam was ambushed near Ben Cat, in a vehicle fitted with direction finding equipment, in 1961, and that, in 1962, the Vietcong found a crashed US aircraft in the Mekong Delta, aboard which were the radios and operator's notes that clearly showed what the role of the aircraft and passengers was. The enemy, in South Vietnam and elsewhere, was well aware of our efforts in this field.

The military manual –
a tidal wave to Melbourne
One day a batch of captured documents arrived at the Divisional Intelligence Unit detachment for translation. These came from 2RAR, which had a NZ Intelligence Officer. Among the items was a request from the Vung Tau City Unit for an Australian Army field manual, and included the ordnance catalogue number, but not the title of the book.

A quick check of ordnance catalogue numbers in the reference book at the detachment did not give a result, so this information was passed across to 1ATF HQ with the other translations. A check of ordnance numbers there included those that were classified 'secret', and there was consternation when the number in the Vietcong letter was for '*Escape and Evasion*'.

There was immediate furore. How did the enemy come to possess such detail of the Australian Army's classified documents? The waves generated went to Vung tau, where some Vietnamese were employed on menial tasks; then to Saigon to Australian HQ there; then to Canberra; then to Melbourne, where the general commanding Ordnance was roused at an early hour and told to investigate. Had disgruntled students somehow found out this information and passed it to the enemy?

Then whispers began.... And grew louder... It became known the letter was sent at the instigation of the NZ IO at 2RAR, and was written by an Aussie linguist.

The Australian hierarchy demanded punishment, but no NZ command was going to inflict anything painful on a NZ officer who had upset the entire Australian military chain from Nui Dat to Melbourne. Presumably he dined out on this story for years.

Bureaucracy –
keeping people in jobs
1RAR had two Australian linguists posted to it for the duration of the tour of duty. In 1966, when the battalion had been in South Vietnam since June 1965, a letter addressed to the commanding officer arrived from the DMI, to inform him that, as in the past twelve months the two had not attended the School to requalify, their status as qualified linguists was in doubt.

Vengeance is a dish
best eaten cold
During the Vietnam War, an Australian battalion commander became very irritated at the RAAF attitude towards the Army's requirements on operations, and at the arbitrary decisions by junior RAAF officers on the basis of their being the pilot in command and so land where they wanted to, and not where required for the operation. He determined that if ever he was in a position to rectify this matter, he would do so.

Years later the opportunity arose. The RAAF persuaded the government that RAAF aircraft could provide all the services and support required by the Defence Force and aircraft carriers would no longer be necessary. Always ready to 'save' money with no thought for the impenetrable future, Australian naval aviation, apart from ship-board anti-submarine matters, ceased to exist.

Expensive new aircraft carriers need not be bought.

This meant that when a proposal was made to the three Service chiefs, Army, Navy and Chief of Defence Force – the battalion commander above - approved transfer of helicopters from RAAF to Army.

Aussie initiative
Though the Australian logistics base at Vung Tau, 1ALSG, was never attacked, the units had to preserve a state of readiness. This included snap night alerts, and 'stand to arms', when the gates would be closed and the defences manned. To practise those involved, an enemy break-in might be included in the event, and the reaction force would go to a designated area to deal with it.

On one night the commander activated the plan and the Reaction Force was sent to a certain part of the defences. The commander went along to watch how this was handled, and waited, but no Reaction Force arrived. And waited.... No Reaction Force. After some time the force was found, nowhere near where it was supposed to be, having been commandeered along the way by a certain sergeant who placed them along his sector of the fence and congratulated himself on his good fortune in having more soldiers than he anticipated.

Obey the road signs
On another night, the 1ALSG Reaction Force became lost in the darkness, having come to a sign denoting road-works, that said, 'No Admittance', did not dare to pass, became lost again, and so could not find its way to the supposed place of enemy activity.

These alerts interfere
with my love life
While access to 1ALSG was supposedly only through the controlled entrance, there actually were many unofficial entry points along the wire, where those people on the staff normally went unofficially into town, to drink and perhaps stay the night with an obliging girlfriend. This was an 'open secret', though perhaps unknown to the senior staff officers.

When stand-to was activated, usually by the 1ALSG siren audible in town, a string of dark figures would be seen walking back, up the slope and through the barbed wire, with a few remarks to those in position.

Vietnamese initiative

The local Vietnamese criminal element soon assessed the capability of the usual defences at 1ALSG and a series of illegal entries was made to steal from the shipping containers inside the fence. They always seemed to know which container had the items desired, cut through the barbed wire, and usually were successful. The plunder was driven away by small cars or the numerous Lambros, which waited on the nearby road.

Sometimes an entire section of wire was cut from between the posts, to make access and removal easier, all done without the 1ALSG garrison being aware anything was happening. One soldier on patrol along the wire did see the big gap, but, despite being in a war zone, accepted it as ongoing repairs that he did not know about. He continued on his way, oblivious to the fact that almost certainly the thieves were nearby in the darkness, quietly waiting to see what he would do.

Cultural differences – 6

Apart from a few who worked in the headquarters in Saigon, the Australians had little opportunity to meet and get to know the Vietnamese, apart from the bar girls, stall owners and similar who lived from the proceeds of bars, restaurants, sale of souvenirs and so on. The wealthy Vietnamese wanted nothing to do with the foreigners, though they did invest in bars and other businesses. There was none of the hospitality extended to foreign servicemen as was extended in the UK 1940-45, or the US and Canada, and in Australia to visiting US service personnel.

Even the local media used different terms when reporting casualties of battle. South Vietnamese dead were presented as having made the supreme sacrifice for the nation, but the foreigners had simply 'died'.

But can you swim?

A nervous RAAF ground crew chap, about to fly from Vung Tau to Saigon in a DeHavilland Caribou twin-engine transport, asked about his parachute, to be assured that the flight would be mainly over water, and if anything happened the pilot would fly as low and as slowly as possible so everyone could jump out safely.

Winning hearts and minds

On Operation 'New Life' in November-December 1965, in Binh Tuy Province, the local Vietcong military commander was captured, by the fortunes of war, in one of the local towns, by a Vietnamese government second class unit. This was a surprise to the US-Australian force on the operation, but the Vietnamese agreed to allow the Australians to have the prisoner for one hour, after which he would be taken back to province headquarters and paraded before the province chief.

The two 1RAR linguists knew they had only that time to acquire anything of use from the Vietcong, as he would disappear into the system. There was absolutely nothing to use for the setting to the interrogation, not even a tent. They took the prisoner to an open area of grass, sat him down and began to politely engage him in conversation, with an offer of a cigarette.

This man looked very much like the famous Chiricahua Apache chief Geronimo: small stature, muscular, with hard facial features, small eyes, slit for a mouth, just like the Apache. DNA now shows that the North American Indians 'Native Americans' are descended from Asians, who crossed from one continent to the other when a definite land bridge existed at Alaska.

The Vietcong commander would talk easily about any subject except military matters; time was passing. The senior Aussie told the other to keep the Vietcong talking while he thought about the problem. After a few moments, the senior signalled he was ready, the other stopped, and the senior told the Vietcong he knew why he had been captured.

This caused the Vietcong to look surprised, and he said, '*Oh; why was I captured?*'

The Aussie said that as the man was the commander, he should have been able to send subordinates in to make a reconnaissance in the town, but he could not trust any of them to do so properly, had to go himself and was captured. The Vietcong was surprised at this, but admitted that it was true.

The Aussie then went on and said that the government forces, who were incompetent in the field, and no match for the Vietcong himself, would torture him at the province capital; agreed. The Aussie went on and said that when he was with the Australians he had been treated politely and respectfully, with no violence, a cigarette and water; agreed, followed with, '*What do you want to know?*'

In the time remaining, the Vietcong told all he knew about his military force, and was passed back to the government forces and their methods.

To add a touch of farce, at the last moment a TV crew came rushing up and asked to film the prisoner. He was asked if he would do a 're-enactment' of his capture, agreed, and went behind a big clump of elephant grass, then came out, hands up, rifle above his head, for the cameras.

Business acumen
By late 1970 the US withdrawal was having an obvious effect on Vietnamese commercial enterprises. At Vung Tau the airfield was no longer as busy as it had been. At the Australian military police unit, the officers and senior NCOs had employed a Vietnamese woman to sweep out the ever-present sand in the accommodation and to do the laundry. The woman chose this moment to demand her payment be doubled, with no negotiation possible. After some discussion, it was decided to do without her services.

We found you at last!
Until the computer revolutionised information storage and retrieval, among other benefits, all military personal files were maintained by hand, with typed or written information added as necessary. After the end of World War 2 in 1945, a number of senior NCOs and Warrant Officers managed to have themselves posted to cosy places, sometimes in small units well away from the major cities, such as ammunition storage depots or supply outfits. With help from a friend in the right place in the central records office, the personal file could be 'lost', misplaced, mis-filed, or simply 'fall' from the cabinet drawer to the space under the files.

One such in Brisbane was the Regular member of a Reserve unit and who remained there for 22 years, so his children were born, educated and left home from the same premises, though many other families endured postings around the nation. When at last it was suggested he go to South Vietnam, he condescended to agree, on the firm understanding at higher headquarters that he would be posted back to the same unit in Brisbane. This was agreed.

In another instance the local townspeople raised a petition to be sent to Army headquarters, asking that 'x' not be sent to South Vietnam as he was the town mayor!

A crown on shoulders
outweighs three stripes
on a sleeve

A rifle company sweeping an area in November 1965 had a succession of small contacts during the day. As evening approached, a contact with one enemy resulted in his death, and an AK47 captured. The significance of this gas-operated automatic weapon was not noted.

Then the Aussies came to an area at the base of a hill where the undergrowth had been cleared, but tree canopy undisturbed, where seating had been made and even lecterns emplaced.

One of the battalion linguists pointed out that this was a 'close training area', just as in the Australian Army, and that the last contact probably had been with a sentry, therefore the enemy now were alert and waiting on the hill-top.

The company commander already had completed a tour of duty as an advisor, and was respected, but strangely he disagreed. There were witnesses to this conversation.

Sure enough, the Vietcong were standing-to on the hill and were well aware of their tactical advantage. The Aussies found themselves in great difficulty, and as night arrived the only feasible thing was to withdraw. Two Aussies were 'missing, believed killed'.

The last two Aussies on the hillside were the company sergeant major and the linguist, who carefully checked the area to make sure no Australians were left, aware that a competent well-armed enemy was very close, and who was exploring the flanks; all in growing darkness. This act of professionalism was never recognised.

The laundry owner

When 1ATF arrived in Phuoc Tuy, it was decided that field uniforms would be laundered at Army expense and a contract was arranged with a laundry in Baria, the province capital. From 1966 until the last Australian units withdrew in October 1971, laundry was done by the civilian business.

Visitors would see the owner, 'mama-san' and her daughters, dressed in the usual Vietnamese pyjama-style blouse and pants, working in the steam-laden shop.

In 1974, a number of senior officers who had served at 1ATF were surprised to be visited by 'mama-san', now very well dressed, hair done, make-up, laden with jewellery, and in the distinctive attractive national dress of Vietnam, the *ao dai*.

There were some calculating looks by spouses when it was explained that the glamourous visitor was 'the laundry lady' from Vietnam.

But mama-san had not come to make trouble. What she wanted was sponsorship to migrate to Australia (it was obvious ARVN could not prevail). Mama-san explained that she was not a penniless refugee who would be a burden on the Australian tax-payer.

She had to documentation to show that for the whole time 1ATF had laundry services provided by her business, no invoices had been presented, and now the Australian government, through Defence, owed her some hundreds of thousands of dollars.

The results
When 1ATF arrived in Phuoc Tuy Province in May 1966, the area was dominated by the Vietcong. The VC 5th Division, of 274 and 275 Regiments, with support units, and a Local Force battalion, D445, plus district and village units and a network of supporting units and groups, regarded the area as home.

1ATF had first to establish a base and then begin to conduct counter-revolutionary warfare operations. The Battle of Long Tan did much to ease pressure on the Aussies, and over time the relentless operations, patrolling and ambushes wore away the enemy presence and effectiveness. The defeats inflicted on the VC/NVA during the Tet 1968 fighting further weakened their appeal to local youth.

The policy of bringing to local town and village market places the bodies of those killed in nearby ambushes and patrol clashes brought home to all the locals the cost of joining the VC.

By 1970 the bigger units had been forced away, the newer D440 was on the point of disbandment. Then D445 split into small groups of about a dozen, totalling only 80 in all, and fled to the distant parts of the province, to grow food and wait for 1ATF to leave. Entire units had ceased to exist.

The situation was such that platoons had areas to patrol, and did so, but some soldiers had been in-country for over nine months and never engaged in battle or even had seen sign of recent enemy presence. Camps found were long abandoned.

1ATF began to reduce in size in 1970 and on the orders of the Australian Prime Minister, William (Billy) McMahon, ceased operations in October 1971. All that remained was an Australian contingent of 100, administering aid projects.

Politics being what it is, when the Australian Labor Party finally won government in December 1972, this commitment was ended and ever-after Labor would boast that 'Whitlam (the prime minister) brought the troops back from Vietnam.' Human nature being what it is, Whitlam never corrected this falsehood.

The Battle of Long Tan
– an alternative version
This 're-locates' the battle into a time when the Greens are involved in politics and the new concept that war can be conducted without violence is in operation.

Historical version.
On 17 August 1966, Vietcong artillery and mortars hit the 1st Australian Task Force (1ATF) base at Nui Dat, Phuoc Tuy Province, South Vietnam. On 18 August the 6th Battalion The Royal Australian Regiment (6RAR) sent rifle companies to search for the firing sites. At the Long Tan rubber plantation 11 Platoon contacted three Vietcong; Sergeant Bob Buick opened fire and D Company 6RAR (D/6RAR) fought the battle that in one afternoon changed the balance of power in the region.

D Company, with expert artillery support of 3,400 rounds controlled by an attached New Zealand artillery officer, Captain Maurie Stanley, held its position against successive assaults, and was reached by a relief force at dusk. Next day and in successive days, over 250 enemy dead were found in the battle area. It was a decisive action, for a loss of 18 Australians killed.

Using the proved historical figure of three or four wounded to one dead in battles, it would be reasonable to estimate that the enemy suffered more dead and some 750 to 1,000 wounded. Another large number would have been necessary to carry the wounded away, plus the weapons and equipment, as only about 100 weapons were found afterwards.

The balance of power in the Australian area of operations changed in that one afternoon to be in favour of 1ATF.

Alternative version,
in a galaxy not so far away.
D/6RAR is warned for the patrol and assembles on the battalion square, 'Peace Plaza'.

As 1ATF Standard Operating Procedures (SOPs) require, before each patrol an officer above company level, in this case, the battalion CO, reads out the Rules Of Engagement (ROE) and platoon commanders collect the statements signed by each man that he has heard and understood the rules.

Also as per SOPs, each man is handed by the platoon sergeants a fresh copy of the card containing the Vietnamese language phrases to be spoken on meeting locals, regardless of the action taken by the local person/s:

'We are your friends from Australia. We respect your culture and cuisine and share your desire for world peace. Come closer and receive gifts of food and medicine.'

All ranks recite the words. A slight disruption at D Company HQ when Private Robin Rencher adds, 'I want to meet your sister.'

Major Harry Smith then moves the company out of 1ATF. D/6 is disgruntled because they will miss the *'Hands Across the Oceans'* concert by The Mormon Tabernacle Choir.

D/6RAR meets B/6RAR hurrying back to the concert. Major Smith deploys the company and 11 Platoon leads into the Long Tan rubber plantation.

Three Vietnamese insurgents walk up to 11 Platoon in a non-aggressive manner, but Sergeant Bob Buick violently opens fire, killing two while the third runs away.

Following 1ATF SOPs, 11 Platoon remains in place and the rest of D/6 arrive. The bodies of the insurgents are untouched, 11 Platoon moves away from the contact site taking care to not disturb the scene, and the brass – expended cartridge cases - from Sergeant Buick's firing is collected and bagged for forensic investigation. As per SOPs, Company Sergeant Major Jack Kirby, D/6RAR, secures Buick's rifle for the investigation.

5RAR in APCs and Chinooks arrives to secure the 11 Platoon contact scene. Royal Australian Corps of Military Police, Special Investigation Branch, legal officers, compensation claims officers, public relations staff, Australian Army Psych teams, Intelligence staff, Red Cross, Amnesty International, Government of Vietnam representatives and media arrive by air – 44 UH-1D sorties are required. The Salvation Army Landrover arrives by road but is sent back to Nui Dat – as per 1ATF SOPs stimulants are forbidden until the investigation is completed. A cup of tea and a biscuit are regarded as inappropriate in such serious proceedings.

11 Platoon is disarmed and removed to Nui Dat for counselling; 2/Lt Gordon Sharp and Sergeant Buick are confined to barracks separately until the interview process is complete. In Australia an Australian Federal Police (AFP) team on standby moves to the airport for deployment to the contact site. They depart for South Vietnam.

The AFP investigation soon shows that Sharp and Buick have different versions of what happened, and on Day Three of the AFP interviews Buick admits that he did not recite the full three sentences of greeting as required, and omitted the second, with 'world peace'.

A sub-investigation begins: how was Buick appointed platoon sergeant while lacking cultural communication skills? CO 6RAR considers his future.

The AFP/Defence report, tabled in Federal Parliament, shows that 2/Lt Sharp did not actually see the three insurgents and that Sergeant Buick acted on his own initiative, but this does not excuse Sharp, Major Smith, battalion commander LtCol Townsend or 1ATF commander Brigadier Jackson. Buick's action in opening fire contravened three UN Resolutions, two Army headquarters directives and the 6RAR Routine Order on cultural sensitivity.

The Prime Minister issued a statement reaffirming Australia's desire for world peace; the Minister for the Army announced that an extra week of training in cultural awareness would be added to the mandatory course at Jungle Training Centre (JTC) Canungra; the Chief of the General Staff (CGS: chief of army) announced that only officer graduates from Duntroon and Portsea military colleges would be permitted to carry live ammunition and this would be issued to soldiers only with approval of Commander 1ATF, or in his absence the senior legal officer 1ATF.

The Leader of the Opposition announced that all Australian workers, students and trade union officers deplored the loss of life and reminded the people of Australia that if returned to office an ALP government would immediately withdraw the Australian military force from South Vietnam and replace it with an equivalent force of trade unionists dedicated to introducing Australian union values to the workers of South Vietnam.

In Phuoc Tuy Province, the insurgents in the Long Tan rubber plantation observed the fast substantial response to the initial contact, realised that their plan to attack the Australian base was disrupted and withdrew to the May Tao mountains to conduct intensive security investigations to identify the traitor. The lone survivor of the contact with 11 Platoon confessed to waving and smiling in a non-revolutionary manner to the Australians.

Major Smith was appointed as SO2 Cultural Affairs at HQ 1st Australian Logistic Support Group (1ALSG), a posting denied by the CGS to be a demotion, but as 'career-broadening'; 2/Lt Sharp was allowed to continue as commander 11 Platoon; Sergeant Buick was posted to the RAAF School of Languages for further training.

The Australian involvement in South Vietnam continued, though the interference by 1ATF in the 1968 Tet celebrations caused further upsets in parliament. Cross-cultural training was increased again.

The Battle of Long Tan
– the aftermath
21 August 1966, Parliament House Canberra; the Senate.
A Greens senator suddenly shrieked, went into hysterics and, sobbing and

moaning, had to be carried from the chamber on a stretcher. Investigation showed the senator had a copy of the report on the Battle of Long Tan and when reading about the role of artillery in the battle, became distressed at the damage to the flora and fauna inflicted by the large number of shells expended, and the long-term effect on the environment around the site.

The Australian Labor Party (ALP) Opposition combined with the Greens, Democrats, independents and a few rebel Country Party representatives to demand an investigation into the effect of artillery on the environment.

The Prime Minister stated that he had never been informed of the effect of artillery, but would not be unhappy to have artillery in his electorate. However, ever-mindful of Australia's international position on preservation of the environment and desire for world peace, he established a bi-partisan committee to investigate and report on the matter within a week.

28 August 1966.
The 'Artillery Committee' tabled its report in Parliament.
Artillery had been found to contribute to unacceptable levels of noise pollution, extensive damage to flora and fauna merely in getting into position to fire its big guns, and the big explosive shells caused huge damage and destruction by the effects of blast and shrapnel to the locations where the shells burst.

Shrapnel was the subject of a supplementary report, in that it was found that much of the shell casing was converted into lumps of hot metal that were propelled over a large area, and merely left there. The committee unanimously recommended that this deplorable attitude to litter on the part of the Army be corrected without delay.

The ministers for the RAAF and RAN discreetly made notes and passed them to their senior public servants.

29 August 1966.
The Prime Minister, Minister for the Army and Minister for Supply stated that they had never been informed of this aspect of artillery use, and that a parliamentary committee would call relevant senior officers to answer questions. The CGS issued a statement that he had been an Engineer and so always was employed on useful construction duties, but Director of Artillery

(DArty) no doubt would be able to explain the matter.

30 August 1966.
DArty informed the committee that Artillery understood the expense to the nation incurred in supply of the heavy vehicles, big guns and expensive ammunition, and would much prefer to keep all this equipment in first-class condition in barracks rather than fire the guns and cause deterioration, wear and the cost of maintenance, but in a caring spirit of collaboration with fellow soldiers, really only ever fired big guns in response to a continuous stream of pleas from the Infantry, who seemed to want expensive shells fired at every opportunity.

DArty said that in the war zone infantry subalterns even requested the guns fire on selected geographical positions as an aid to cross-country navigation. (Greens senator collapsed on hearing this; adjournment while psychological assistance provided.)

Director of Infantry admitted that subalterns sometimes did call for a round of artillery to fall at a location as an aid to navigation, but this was unofficial and could have been stopped by Artillery refusing to fire, though in his experience the gunners loved to fire, but no amount of practice seemed to improve their accuracy, for which they blamed all sorts of airy-fairy things collectively titled ballistics.

Anyway, DInf went on, the infantry was very thoughtful and caring in its movements through and use of the environment, and every soldier was required to observe the 'burn, bash and bury' policy.

The Greens senator had just returned to the room and again collapsed when this was explained. The Green/Democrat alliance issued a statement denouncing the widespread damage caused: 'burn' released noxious fumes which attacked the ozone layer, 'bash' ingrained the use of violence in the military; 'bury' disturbed the natural state of the ground and introduced foreign matter into it, so constituting a hazard to the normal life forms in the region.

2 September 1966.
The Prime Minister announced that, after due consideration, the CGS had been instructed to disband the Artillery (RAA), but to replace it with the

Arbour Service (AS); all the big guns would be sold for scrap; 50% of RAA vehicles and men would be transferred to AS and a nation-wide program of tree-planting employing AS would begin.

The new AS corps badge would be a symbolic tree with 'Ubique' at the base, all surrounded by a floral wreath. Greens demanded that endangered species be included in the design.

Returned Services League national office announced that a Guard would be mounted on the memorial gun outside every RSL to prevent removal.

Natural justice would be served in that the Infantry would search for, collect and arrange transport of all shrapnel previously scattered in training areas in Australia and overseas battle areas such as Long Tan. The establishments of Infantry, RAASC (service corps) and RAAOC (ordnance) units would be increased to cope by absorbing the other 50% of RAA.

Director of Infantry was reported as saying that the dogs of Australia would be glad of the extra trees, but this was later denied, and that DInf really had used military terminology and said that 'Foxhound' elements would be glad of the trees for camouflage and concealment.

A spokesperson for the Greens/Democrats/Socialist collective said the trees were not for the use of soldiers, but for peace-loving poets, students and workers and trade union picnic parties.

The Rats of Tobruk Association issued a statement saying that today's young soldiers knew nothing about fighting in a real war, and at Tobruk the Diggers did not need trees to hide behind when they gave old Rommel the fright of his life. No trees, a good field of fire and cold steel were the answers; the Association supported Artillery in all its forms and suggested Engineers be employed to remove trees to assist the Infantry.

The Kokoda Association agreed and said the trees in Papua New Guinea were a damned nuisance in 1942-43, and that poker machine profits would be diverted to supply chain-saws for every unit in South Vietnam.

Greens and Democrats denounced this, and announced they would go to South Vietnam to conduct an inventory of trees in Phuoc Tuy Province, and would hold frequent inspections to check their continued survival. Individual trees would be sponsored by school students across Australia. The (ALP) Opposition urged that military maps include the locations of all endangered species and that all ranks be issued a copy before operations.

3 September 1966.
The CGS called in his SO1 (Personnel) and reminded him that this whole blasted business was caused by those fellows in D Company 6RAR, and to arrange for the D/6RAR officers and NCOs to be posted at once, unaccompanied, to that place in Tasmania where the boffins were researching field rations.

The scientists had requested a detachment of 100 people of any rank for two years to provide corporate continuity, and at the moment were about to begin testing something described as 'spicy prune omelette with castor oil dressing' as an answer to constipation in the field.

Printed in Great Britain
by Amazon

78681082R00075